· T 4

Road Library
Road

11 JUL 1981
13. AUG. 1981
10. MAY 1983
11 MAY 1984
-7 DEC 1984

AUG. 1980

ROUGH OF ENFIELD
RY SERVICES

ED on or before the latest date stamped
een obtained by personal call, post or
above number and the date due for return.

The Fourth Man

The Fourth Man

The Story of Blunt, Philby, Burgess and Maclean

Douglas Sutherland

Secker & Warburg London

First published in England 1980 simultaneously by
Martin Secker & Warburg Limited
54 Poland Street, London WIV 3DF
and Arrow Books Limited
3 Fitzroy Square, London WI

Copyright © 1980 by Douglas Sutherland

SBN: 436 50600 9

Printed in Great Britain by The Anchor Press Ltd
and bound by Wm Brendon & Son Ltd
both of Tiptree, Essex

London Borough
of Enfield
Public Libraries

T 41147

Contents

	Acknowledgments	7
	Chronology	8
	Introduction	17
1	The Craft of Espionage	21
2	Assorted Adolescents	31
3	The Cambridge Connection	43
4	Postgraduates	50
5	The War	62
6	The Cold War	71
7	The Plot Unfolds	89
8	Day of Departure	100
9	And Now, Melinda	110
10	Paperchase	119
11	Eleven Years After	129
12	The Third Man	136
13	The Fourth Man	143
14	The Old Boys' Reunion	157
15	What Did They Do For Russia?	162
	Index	169

I wish to acknowledge my debt to the very large number of people who have contributed to this book. Too many to list have helped me with personal reminiscences, either in 1962 when I was researching BURGESS AND MACLEAN, published by Secker & Warburg in 1963 with my co-author Anthony Purdy, or in the few hectic weeks that I have spent without, alas, a co-author to help me, in preparing this new book.

I have either quoted directly or used material from the following books:

The Missing Diplomats, by Cyril Connolly (Queen Anne Press) 1953
The Missing Macleans, by Geoffrey Hoare (Cassell) 1955
The Great Spy Scandal, edited by John Mather and Donald Seaman (Daily Express) 1955
Guy Burgess: A Portrait With Background, by Tom Driberg (Weidenfeld & Nicolson) 1956
An Autobiography, by Herbert Morrison (Odham's Press) 1960
Kim Philby: The Spy I Loved, by Eleanor Philby (Pan Books) 1968
My Silent War, by H. A. R. Philby (MacGibbon & Kee) 1968
Philby, by Bruce Page, David Leitch, Philip Knightley (André Deutsch) 1968
A Chapter of Accidents, by Goronwy Rees (Chatto & Windus) 1972
Chronicles of Wasted Time, Volumes 1 and 2, by Malcolm Muggeridge (Collins) 1972 and 1973
Philby, by Patrick Seale and Maureen McCouville (Hamish Hamilton) 1973
John Strachey, by Hugh Thomas (Eyre Methuen) 1973
Most Secret War, by R. V. Jones (Hamish Hamilton) 1978
Inside Story, by Chapman Pincher (Sidgwick & Jackson) 1978
The Climate of Treason, by Andrew Boyle (Hutchinson) 1979
Who's Who (A. & C. Black) 1979

and am indebted to all the authors and publishers for permission to use quotations and benefit from new insights.

My thanks also to my *chef de bureau* Henrietta Davies-Cook and to Adam Shand-Kydd for valuable research.

Douglas Sutherland

Chronology

	ANTHONY BLUNT BORN 1907	H. A. R. (KIM) PHILBY BORN 1912	GUY BURGESS BORN 1912	DONALD MACLEAN BORN 1911	PRIME MINISTERS AND FOREIGN SECRETARIES
1928		Undergraduate Trinity College Cambridge	Eton College	Gresham's Holt School	PM S. Baldwin FS Sir A. Chamberlain
1929	Trinity College	Undergraduate Trinity College Cambridge. Joins University Socialist Society	Eton College	Undergraduate Trinity Hall Cambridge	PM J. R. MacDonald 8 June FS A. Henderson
1930	Trinity College Joins Apostles		Trinity College	Trinity Hall. Professes Communism	As above
1931	Trinity College. Graduates		Trinity College. Joins anti-war movement.	Trinity Hall	PM J. R. MacDonald FS Marquis of Reading
1932	Appointed a Don Trinity College		Trinity College. Professes Communism. Joins Apostles	Trinity Hall	As above

Becomes Treasurer University Socialist Society

ANTHONY BLUNT BORN 1907	H. A. R. (KIM) PHILBY BORN 1912	GUY BURGESS BORN 1912	DONALD MACLEAN BORN 1911	PRIME MINISTERS AND FOREIGN SECRETARIES
1933 Don at Trinity. Visit to Moscow	Leaves University. Goes to Vienna and converted to Communism	Trinity College. Nervous breakdown. Gets aegrotat degree	Trinity Hall	PM J. R. MacDonald FS Sir J. Simon
1934 Sabbatical year mostly studying architecture in Rome	Marries Austrian Jewish Communist Litzi Kohlman. Joins Anglo-German Fellowship and apparently denounces Communism	Postgraduate year at Cambridge. Refuses offer of Fellowship. Visits Moscow	Trinity Hall. Gets 2nd class degree in Modern Languages	As above
1935 Cambridge. Burgess recruits to Comintern	London. Working for *Review of Reviews*	Works for Mrs Rothschild. Apparent conversion to National Socialism and works for Col. Macnamara MP	Passes Foreign Office Examination	PM S. Baldwin 7 June FS Sir S. Hoare
1936 Leaves Cambridge. Takes post with Warburg Institute, London		Joins BBC Talks Department	Foreign Office in London	PM S. Baldwin FS Sir A. Eden

ANTHONY BLUNT BORN 1907	H. A. R. (KIM) PHILBY BORN 1912	GUY BURGESS BORN 1912	DONALD MACLEAN BORN 1911	PRIME MINISTERS AND FOREIGN SECRETARIES
1937	Reader, History of Art, London University. Deputy Director, Courtauld Institute of Art	Joins *The Times* and sent as correspondent Spanish Civil War on Franco's side	BBC, running programme 'The Week in Westminster'. Visits Philby in Spain	Foreign Office in London	PM N. Chamberlain 28 May FS Sir A. Eden
1938	Continues as above	In Spain. Awarded 'Red Cross of Military Merit' presented personally by Franco	BBC as above. Meeting with Churchill. Leaves BBC to join section 'D', war office	Posted as Third Secretary, British Embassy, Paris	As above
1939	At outbreak of war called up. Intelligence Corps. 48 hours later reposted Field Intelligence – in France promoted Captain	From Spain to France as war correspondent (September)	As above	British Embassy, Paris	PM N. Chamberlain FS Viscount Halifax

	ANTHONY BLUNT BORN 1907	H. A. R. (KIM) PHILBY BORN 1912	GUY BURGESS BORN 1912	DONALD MACLEAN BORN 1911	PRIME MINISTERS AND FOREIGN SECRETARIES
1940	Escapes France losing half of his section. Enlisted in MI5 London	Enlisted by Burgess in Grand's 'D' Section. Later transferred SOE	Fired from Section 'D' after enlisting Philby	Marries Melinda and escapes France as Paris falls	PM W. S. Churchill 11 May FS Sir A. Eden
1941	Junior position with MI5 London	SOE first tutor at spy school, Beaulieu. Joins MI6 Section V, London	Returns to BBC. Runs programme 'Can I Help You'	Foreign Office London exempt from military service	As above
1942	As above	Section V of MI6 moves to St Albans. Extended responsibility. Marries second wife Aileen	As above	As above	As above
1943	As above	Section V. Returns London. Concerned with counter-espionage Germany, Italy etc.	Restless at BBC	As above, with increased responsibilities of Second Secretary	As above
1944	As above. Marginally greater responsibility	Appointed head of new department Section IX, to operate against Communism and Soviet Union	Transfers to News Department Foreign Office and passes entrance examination	Posted British Embassy Washington. Promoted First Secretary	As above

	ANTHONY BLUNT BORN 1907	H. A. R. (KIM) PHILBY BORN 1912	GUY BURGESS BORN 1912	DONALD MACLEAN BORN 1911	PRIME MINISTERS AND FOREIGN SECRETARIES
1945	MI5 London. Promoted Surveyor of King's Pictures (George VI)	Volkov threatens to talk and implicate Philby	News Department Foreign Office	British Embassy Washington. Promoted Counsellor and Head of Chancery	PM W. S. Churchill PM C. R. Attlee 26 July FS E. Bevin 27 July
1946		First field appointment – Head of Turkish MI6 service.	Joins Private Office of Hector McNeil, Minister of State, Foreign Office	British Embassy, Washington. Secretary Atomic Energy Committee	As above
1947	As above. Mission for King to Germany. Director, Courtauld Institute of Art	As above. 'Cover' job. First Secretary, British Embassy	As above	British Embassy Washington, as above	As above
1948	As above. Commander of Order of Orange Nassau	As above	Appointed Far Eastern Department, Foreign Office	As above	As above

	ANTHONY BLUNT BORN 1907	H. A. R. (KIM) PHILBY BORN 1912	GUY BURGESS BORN 1911	DONALD MACLEAN BORN 1911	PRIME MINISTERS AND FOREIGN SECRETARIES
1949	Surveyor of King's Pictures. Director of Courtauld Institute of Art	Appointed to Washington as top MI6 officer to liaise with CIA and FBI. On committee for Albanian operation	Foreign Office	Posted Cairo as Head of Chancery. Drinking bouts intensified. Melinda gives dinner party for HRH the Duke of Edinburgh	PM C. R. Attlee FS E. Bevin
1950	As above	British Embassy, Washington. Puts up Burgess at his house	Posted to British Embassy, Washington. Disciplinary troubles	Posted London – breakdown, sick leave. Then Head of American Department, Foreign Office	PM C. R. Attlee FS H. M. Morrison
1951	As above. Questioned by MI5	Recalled to London. Interrogated over Burgess and Maclean affair, asked to resign	Returned to London in disgrace and suspended from duty. 25 May vanishes	Under surveillance. 25 May vanishes with Burgess	PM Sir W. S. Churchill 26 October FS Sir A. Eden 28 October
1952	Surveyor of Queen's Pictures. Director of Courtauld Institute of Art	June: lengthy and severe interrogation by Milmo	Whereabouts officially unknown	Whereabouts officially unknown	As above

	ANTHONY BLUNT BORN 1907	H. A. R. (KIM) PHILBY BORN 1912	GUY BURGESS BORN 1912	DONALD MACLEAN BORN 1911	PRIME MINISTERS AND FOREIGN SECRETARIES
1953	Surveyor of Queen's Pictures. Director of Courtauld Institute. Periodical questioning	Fallow but not officially dismissed	Whereabouts unknown	Whereabouts unknown. Family disappear from Switzerland	PM Sir W. S. Churchill FS Sir A. Eden
1954	As above	As above	As above	As above	
1955	As above	Question in House of Commons asked by Marcus Lipton. Harold Macmillan officially clears but Philby dismissed from MI6	White Paper on disappearance. Destination Moscow 'assumed'	White Paper on disappearance. Destination Moscow 'assumed'	PM Sir A. Eden 6 April FS H. Macmillan 7 April
1956	Knighted by HM the Queen	September – goes to Beirut as correspondent for *The Observer* and *The Economist*	Russians admit is in Moscow. Gives Press Conference	Russians admit is in Moscow. Gives Press Conference	PM Sir A. Eden FS H. Macmillan
1957	Questioning continues	Aileen, second wife, dies	Tom Driberg publishes biography	Moscow	PM H. Macmillan 13 January FS Selwyn Lloyd 14 January

Year	ANTHONY BLUNT BORN 1907	H. A. R. (KIM) PHILBY BORN 1912	GUY BURGESS BORN 1912	DONALD MACLEAN BORN 1911	PRIME MINISTERS AND FOREIGN SECRETARIES
1958	Awarded French Légion d'Honneur	Marries Eleanor Brewer	Moscow, with companion Tolya	Moscow	As above
1959	Questioning continues	Beirut	Moscow. Privileges gradually withdrawn	Moscow	PM H. Macmillan FS Selwyn Lloyd
1960	As above	As above	As above	As above	PM H. Macmillan FS Lord Home 27 July
1961	As above	As above	Threat to return scares authorities	As above	As above
1962	As above	George Blake caught. Philby now known as KGB agent	Warrant for arrest issued United Kingdom	Warrant for arrest issued United Kingdom	As above
1963	As above	Nicholas Elliott flies out to interrogate. 23 January disappears. 1 June named as 'Third Man' – takes Russian citizenship	Purdy and Sutherland publish book pointing to Blunt as Third/Fourth Man. Burgess dies – ashes flown home	Purdy and Sutherland publish book pointing to Blunt as Third/Fourth Man	PM Sir A. Douglas-Home 19 October FS R. A. Butler 20 October

	ANTHONY BLUNT BORN 1907	H. A. R. (KIM) PHILBY BORN 1912	GUY BURGESS BORN 1912	DONALD MACLEAN BORN 1911	PRIME MINISTERS AND FOREIGN SECRETARIES
1964	Alleged confession of guilt to MI5. Guaranteed immunity	De-briefing by KGB completed		Moscow	PM H. Wilson 16 October FS P. Gordon-Walker 16 October
1965	As above	Awarded 'Red Banner of Honour' by USSR		As above	PM H. Wilson FS M. Stewart 22 June
1968		Publishes autobiography		As above	PM H. Wilson FS M. Stewart
1979	Prime Minister names him Fourth Man. H.M. the Queen withdraws knighthood	Promoted to KGB General		As above	PM M. Thatcher 4 May FS Lord Carrington 8 May

Introduction

On Thursday 15 November 1979, the Labour Member of Parliament Mr Ted Leadbitter had a question down for answer by the Prime Minister, Mrs Thatcher: 'Will she make a statement on recent evidence concerning the actions of an individual, whose name has been supplied to her, in relation to the security of the United Kingdom.'

The name was already generally known, because the Hansard for 15 November contained the text of a question from Christopher Price, MP, to Sir Michael Havers, the Attorney-General, which was down to be answered on the following Monday. Price was asking whether the file on Sir Anthony Blunt would be referred to the Director of Public Prosecutions in connection with the case of Burgess and Maclean. Mrs Thatcher's written answer to Mr Leadbitter started: 'The name which the Honourable Gentleman has given me is that of Sir Anthony Blunt . . .'

Although she went on to elaborate, her first sentence was enough to set off one of the greatest spy sensations of the century.

There were several people to whom the Prime Minister's information did not come as a complete surprise. One of them was Sir Anthony Blunt himself. At 10.30 am on the previous day, the Secretary to the Cabinet, Sir Robert Armstrong, had telephoned Blunt's solicitor, Mr Michael Rubinstein, and informed him that the question would be asked the following day and that the Prime Minister would, as a result, disclose Sir Anthony's guilt . . .

One man who read the intended Commons question was Ed Boyle, political correspondent for the London Broadcasting Company and son of Mr Andrew Boyle, whose recently published book *The*

Climate of Treason had led to renewed speculation over the circumstances surrounding the disappearance of Foreign Office diplomats Burgess and Maclean some twenty-eight years earlier. Young Mr Boyle at once picked up the telephone and called his father. 'I think you had better be in the House this afternoon,' he told him. Thus it was that Andrew Boyle was in the Strangers' Gallery to hear Mrs Thatcher rip the veil of secrecy off the identity of the spy whom the Official Secrets Act had forced him to name only as 'Maurice' in his book. His reaction was one of stunned surprise that so many details had been given. It was a reaction shared by me.

In 1963, when Anthony Purdy and I published our book *Burgess and Maclean*, we had known with complete certainty that the shadowy figure now known in the popular numbers game as 'The Fourth Man' was Sir Anthony Blunt. So sure of this had I become in the course of the researches that we carried out in 1962 that I asked Blunt for a meeting. It took place over a drink in the Travellers' Club. I gave him my reasons for believing him to be extensively implicated. The news was obviously a terrible shock to him. He had come to the club, I suppose, expecting to be asked for details of the period when he and Burgess had shared a flat but I was probably the first person, apart from various MI5 officials, who had openly accused him of being a part of the spy ring. Of course he denied it and claimed that Guy's defection had been as much of a shock to him as to anyone else. This I now know to be true. Unfortunately I did not realize at the time just how the last minute tipoff to Maclean had been contrived and wrongly accused Blunt of using his MI5 contacts to tell Maclean on Friday that he was to be interrogated on he Monday after his flight. This, it now emerges, was not the case. My inadvertent disclosure that my information was not entirely accurate seemed to rally Blunt. He stopped shaking and mumbling, told me in a comparatively firm voice that I would hear from his solicitors immediately if his name appeared anywhere in connection with the case, and beat a hasty retreat.

When Anthony Purdy and I researched and published our book in 1962 and 1963 restrictions under the Official Secrets Act were more stringent than they are today. Few people in the Establishment were anxious to risk 'guilt by association' by admitting that they had been friends of either man. Philby was still in Beirut and Blunt had not yet made his confession. Nevertheless I must admit that we had certain advantages over later writers in the field. The more obvious advantage was that many of those involved were still alive. Even those who can still be questioned were able to remember the part they played in events that much more clearly in those days.

When writing his admirably researched *The Climate of Treason*, Andrew Boyle shared with us the inestimable advantage of having the cooperation of Mr Goronwy Rees, whose personal knowledge of Burgess's activities was probably unequalled either outside or inside the ranks of the professionals. Sadly, Rees died of cancer shortly after Boyle's book was published.

In 1962, however, Purdy and I had other important sources open to us. The late Tom Driberg had written what many were tempted to call the authorized Burgess biography. I once incurred his displeasure by remarking, half in jest, that I considered that he had written nothing but the plain varnished truth. It was an unfair jibe, and particularly ungenerous to Tom, who gave us many extremely interesting pieces of background information that he had thought it unwise to publish. Tom was a loyal friend to Burgess, but the fact that he went to Moscow to check over the book (*Guy Burgess: A Portrait with Background*) and subsequently had it vetted by the security authorities does not mean that it was a 'whitewash'. It remains the most authoritative book on Burgess to this day.

There were many others in the Foreign Office and in both MI5 and MI6, who had known either or both of them before their flight to Moscow, who provided welcome clues. Others, perhaps even more important, amongst those to whom we talked were closely connected with one or other in their private lives. Contrary to the impression later given by the newspapers, we found that Burgess and Maclean moved in entirely different circles and had very few friends in common.

At the same time we also laboured under certain disadvantages. Homosexuality was still an indictable offence, so that we had to get involved in such fatuous circumlocutions as describing the late Sir Harold Nicolson as 'a well-known writer'. To have named him would have been to risk a libel suit. The Official Secrets Act and the laws of libel caused us as much trouble as they did Andrew Boyle. In 1962 the Establishment had perhaps closed ranks rather more tightly than eighteen years later. Certainly there was no one then in high political office to play the role of Margaret Thatcher.

On balance, however, I still feel that we had the easier task. I knew Maclean slightly and Burgess well. I rather liked Burgess, if only because he could always be relied upon to be not only outrageous but amusing. It is because he was so colourful that he is often wrongly regarded as the most serious defector of them all. In the chapters that follow I have relied heavily on the material Purdy and I collected for *Burgess and Maclean*. We were unable to use a lot of it then, but much more of the story can now not only be fitted into the jigsaw but, thanks to Mrs Thatcher, published.

Equally I owe a lot to material subsequently unearthed by other writers whom I have duly acknowledged at the beginning of this book. I cannot pretend that the present text is entirely accurate, but I hope it will provide a useful guide for those who want to know who the Four Men were, what they did and when they did it. More important, perhaps, I hope it will help to put the whole affair into some sort of perspective.

That I could not aspire to complete accuracy was obvious from the outset. Unless and until the various secret organizations in England, America and Russia open their unedited files to public scrutiny, much must remain a matter for deduction and speculation.

But apart from matters which are legitimately government secrets, I have been highly amused, in the course of my 1979 researches, to note the differences (some of them quite substantial) which occur in eye-witness accounts of incidents given by the same person to different authors on different dates. The human memory, alas, is fallible. Where I have noticed such contradictions I have quoted the version given to me. It may not be the best account of the incident available, but at least it is an accurate transcription of what someone who was there at the time told me in 1962.

1 The Craft of Espionage

That the Blunt exposure should result in the whole of Fleet Street going spy-mad was predictable. There is nothing more titillating to the public imagination than a good spy story. It has been so since long before the siege of Troy, and will continue to be so long after the Statue of Liberty on Staten Island has crumbled into dust. All of us to some degree are spies at heart. The little old lady in Acacia Road peeping out from behind her lace curtains to observe the comings and goings of her neighbours is indulging in a little personal espionage. At the other end of the scale in the private sector there are few big businesses who do not deem it both prudent and profitable to keep a close eye on the activities of their competitors. In big business, industrial espionage is big business.

When I was in the army there was a well known adage which was drummed into all ranks. It was: 'Time spent on reconnaissance is seldom wasted.' Not even the most foolhardy when-in-doubt-gallop commander, with the possible exception of Lord Cardigan at Balaclava, would question the wisdom of knowing as much as possible about enemy strengths and weaknesses before launching an attack.

It is only when governments become involved in the cloak and dagger business that the whole thing takes on a delicious air of disrepute. It is a matter for public outrage if a traitor is found within our gates, and a matter of great satisfaction when one of 'them' comes over to 'our' side.

It should not be assumed that masters of the spy thriller such as Graham Greene, John le Carré or Len Deighton are blessed with unusually vivid imaginations. On the contrary, they are probably more accurate reporters of the spy scene than romantic novelists are of affairs of the heart. The spy business at the sharp end is indeed the very stuff of drama. The rewards can be great and the penalty for failure terminal. This is not to say that the main business of any country's espionage service is not an unglamorous desk job of breaking cyphers and sifting a mass of evidence which may or may not be relevant.

In the light of this let us examine the general attitude towards espionage. In the more or less immediate past there have been various *causes célèbres* which linger on in the popular imagination. The Dreyfus case so dramatically exposed by the efforts of one man, Emile Zola, was a spy story in the classic tradition – that it was also seen as a demonstration of anti-semitism which led to a monstrous miscarriage of justice should not obscure that fact.

There can be few even amongst the youth of today who do not react positively to the real-life drama of the glamorous sex spy as epitomized by Mata Hari, or who do not relate to the gallantry of Nurse Edith Cavell in the First World War, or of Odette Churchill in the Second.

This may go some way towards explaining why the names of Burgess and Maclean, Philby and now Blunt should be as indelibly associated in our Island Story as Stanley and Livingstone, Morecambe and Wise or Fortnum and Mason.

What has separated them from the bigger fish in the espionage aquarium, and what everybody seems to find so unforgivable, is that they were palpably 'upper-class'. For an old Borstal boy to be unmasked as a traitor to his country is, in the public mind, understandable and even forgivable. To be an Old Boy from Eton (Burgess), Marlborough (Blunt), Westminster (Philby) or even an alumnus from such a minor public school as Gresham's (Maclean) makes them instantly more interesting and predictably more suitable targets for the righteously indignant. The fact that they all went on to be Cambridge undergraduates and afterwards to become minor pillars of the Establishment makes their crime more heinous still.

In 1950, one year before Burgess and Maclean slipped across the Channel on their way to Moscow, the distinguished British physicist Alan Nunn May had been given a long prison sentence and was dubbed both a traitor to his country and a spy for a foreign power. In the general view justice had been done and honour satisfied. Nunn May's crime was indeed serious. He freely confessed not only to handing over to the Russians the formula for the production of uranium 235, but also of sending them a free sample of the material. It is hard to imagine anything more serious.

And yet... One of the few occasions on which I met Sir Winston Churchill, other than briefly, was when I was invited to lunch with him by Mr Raymond Blackburn, possibly the most brilliant, if the most erratic, of the Labour MPs elected in 1945. The subject of Nunn May's prison sentence was the main topic of conversation. Blackburn, who took a close interest in nuclear developments, dilated at some length on the subject whilst Sir Winston listened with what I considered at the time to be considerable patience.

Blackburn's theme was that Alan Nunn May was not motivated by greed or by communist affiliations. He was (and I am satisfied that this is correct) an idealist who felt that the fact that Professor Rutherford had done all the important research on uranium 235 did not give the British the sole right to the results of his researches. Nunn May thought it our duty to share such knowledge with our allies – and however artificial our alliance with Russia at the time, politically speaking, we were allies. Blackburn argued that whilst Nunn May's conviction and sentence was necessary, if only *pour décourager les autres*, he should not go down in history as a spy or a traitor but rather as an idealist.

Winston Churchill took some time to consider this seemingly untenable point of view, and then delivered himself of a particularly Churchillian judgement. As I remember it his exact words were: 'Your argument, Raymond, is not without merit. It may well be that Mr Nunn May has done our country some service, if only in maintaining the Balance of Terror.'

What Churchill so dramatically described as 'maintaining the Balance of Terror' may be described as the daily bread and butter of the spy business.

The Blunt scandal has led to a great deal of wild speculation as to how many other spies there were connected with the Cambridge four at large inside the Establishment. Andrew Boyle has been quoted as believing that there were around twenty.

'M', James Bond's master spy, was a figure drawn from life by his creator, Ian Fleming. There are Ms sitting behind large desks in every politically sensitive capital in the world. The number of people actively involved in spying or supervising and controlling spies is legion. In many cases spies or agents become double agents, and when they are known to be double agents they sometimes become triple agents for a time. It is the spy-master's job to feed his double agents with information to be passed on to the other side, and to assess the value of the information the double agent is able to give him in return. Both sides may be aware of the situation, but it is sometimes as important to know what the other side want us to believe as it is to find out what they do not want us to know. It is only when it is decided that a double or triple agent is being of more value to 'them' than to 'us' that a decision has to be taken about how he should be rendered ineffective.

The ways of doing this are many and varied. In the case of the smaller fry it is a matter of cutting off the supply of money and information and warning them of the penalties of continued cooperation with their connections on the other side. More important spies, holding, for instance, high positions in the Foreign Service as their cover, would probably be pulled in for rigorous interrogation in order to discover how much damage they had done. It is relatively seldom in any Secret Service that agents in this category are put on trial. Even trial *in camera* does not guarantee that evidence will not be given which might embarrass the organization concerned.

Trials *in camera* serve a useful purpose in protecting the reputations of innocent witnesses called to give evidence in ordinary criminal proceedings (blackmail cases, for example). They are very far from being equally effective when matters of national security are involved. Any trial in England entails the accused being charged in open court with the offences alleged. The prosecution may then ask for the proceedings to be conducted *in camera* in the interests of national security, but already much of the damage has been done. If, for example, the accused is known to be a high official in the Foreign Service, public curiosity and unease is aroused.

During the course of the trial a large number of people are of necessity involved. There are of course the jury as well as the judge, counsel and court officials. It would be naive indeed to assume that all would be discreet. In the course of the trial the comings and goings of the various witnesses, whose identity proceedings *in camera* are specifically designed to protect, can be easily observed from the steps of the Old Bailey by an interested party. Thus the cover of agents can be compromised. At the same time an enemy agent to whom it might be alleged secret information has been passed is very often under diplomatic immunity but could not, in any case, be subpoenaed to give evidence. If they were in fact spying for their governments, what chance is there that they would tell the truth and implicate one of their own agents just because they were on oath?

This explains the very proper reluctance of our Secret Services to put spy masters as opposed to field agents on trial – the damage it might do would be much greater than any advantage it might achieve. There is the further consideration that, although the 'proof' against, for instance, Maclean and Blunt satisfied MI5, there is a strong possibility that it would have left the average jury with a reasonable doubt.

Whilst this may be generally accepted, it is obviously proper to inquire why the men who gave the Russians the formula for the atom bomb: Klaus Fuchs, Bruno Pontecorvo and Alan Nunn May, should be exposed to public trial and subjected to the severest penalities for their treachery, if caught, while Blunt, Philby, Burgess and Maclean were not.

To answer that question it is necessary to understand the difference between an agent in the field, working for whichever side, and a desk man. The former is employed exclusively, and frequently extremely lucratively, to provide highly secret information in a limited field for an enemy power. He, or in many cases she, falls into the same category as a spy caught working for the enemy in time of war, who knows that the penalty for failure is to be put up against a wall and shot. Field agents in this category are seldom, if ever, in a position to compromise the organization that employs them. They have one or two contacts they might betray, but know little of the headquarters that gives them their orders. They started work with the knowledge that they could expect no intervention from their own side in the event of detection and no mercy from their victims. The evidence against field agents can generally be reduced to terms a jury will be able to understand. Proof of documents photographed and furtively disposed of, for instance.

George Blake is a good example. He traded not in military secrets but in selling out to the enemy the names of his fellow field agents serving throughout Europe. This was rightly regarded as the ultimate in treachery and his sentence to forty-two years' imprisonment reflects this view. Other political regimes would not have been so merciful. The Russian General Krevitsky, a defector of immense importance to the Americans in 1937, was found murdered in a seedy hotel room in New York in 1941. From time to time other defectors from behind the Iron Curtain, like the unfortunate Bulgarian, Georgi Markov, injected with a tiny poisoned capsule through the tip of an umbrella in a London street, briefly become headline news.

Headquarters men or desk agents present different problems. Often their role is not to supply copies of official documents but to give their masters summaries or assessments of situations. Again they have legitimate as well as clandestine reasons for meeting representatives of the foreign power they work for. Finally, they are rarely paid. Proof of treason is thus infinitely more difficult to establish than in the case of agents in the field. Moreover, if proof can be collected, it will probably involve the disclosure of sensitive official secrets. These secrets are, of course, known to the power who employed the agent but this is very much less damaging than its becoming public knowledge.

In the light of this it may be of interest to give an assessment of the importance of the desk agents, Burgess, Blunt, Maclean and Philby.

Anybody who knew Burgess must quickly have realized that in the espionage hierarchy he was very small fry indeed. In fact it is probable that our Secret Services did not regard him as a spy at all in the true sense of the word. In any event there is little evidence that the Russians made much use of him after 1939.

If Burgess were alive to read this there is little doubt that it would make him very angry indeed. Guy Burgess desperately wanted to be a spy and assiduously cultivated anyone in the spying business, regardless of whether they were Russian, American or members of our own Secret Service. He frequently gave expression to his frustration that nobody would employ him by saying to anyone whom he wished to impress things like: 'Surely you realize that I am a Comintern agent' – hardly the sort of remark likely to make anybody take him seriously. His ultimate gesture in defecting with Maclean was a matter of complete indifference to the Foreign Office, who had already suspended him from duty for his personal behaviour and who did not believe the Russians would find him useful.

Blunt too was of relative unimportance. It may be that his role as self-confessed recruiter of spies during his Cambridge days has been underestimated, but as he was known to have communist sympathies at the beginning of the war, it is hardly credible that he was given access to information of great significance. This is not to say that he was incapable of being a thoroughgoing traitor, but only to show that his importance is diminished by the modicum of damage he was able to do. His role with regard to the disappearance to Russia of Burgess and Maclean and later Philby will be seen in perspective when we come to consider the matter later. The Russians were our allies in the war against Germany for most of the years he worked for MI5, and his activities as an art historian cannot have been of much interest to the Kremlin.

Maclean was a rather different kettle of fish. Unlike Burgess, who during his diplomatic career had never risen from the second rank, Donald Maclean had done well. He was in the senior branch of the service, and his post as First Secretary at our Embassy in Washington was one which was generally accepted as the springboard to higher things. He undoubtedly had access to information of high security value while he was in America, and he equally undoubtedly passed such information to the Russians. But Maclean had personality defects, although not on such a serious scale as Burgess, and these fortunately limited his usefulness.

In Philby, however, we have somebody who has to be taken far more seriously than either Burgess, Blunt or Maclean. He held an exceedingly high rank in MI6, had set up the section that spied on the Soviet Union, and at the same time was held in equal regard by the KGB. How far and for how long his contribution to maintaining the Balance of Terror was known to us or how much harm he did is something that it is impossible to evaluate. It is, however, certain that under no circumstances could we have afforded to put *him* on trial. He was a man of immense ambition, hungry for power and with a mental dexterity which made him a very formidable character to deal with indeed. He might well have convinced a jury that he was the innocent victim of a witch hunt. . . .

By and large the climate of opinion following Burgess and Maclean's disappearance was one that was sharply critical of the ineptness, inefficiency and naiveté of the Foreign Office and of our Secret Services.

Whilst the defection of Burgess and Maclean caused a shake-up in MI5 and MI6, instigated by Herbert Morrison under the Prime Ministership of Clement Attlee, most of the Press accusations were probably unduly harsh.

The British Secret Services, rather like the Royal Family, are in no position to defend themselves against unfair criticism; moreover the most virulent criticism is apt to come from the least informed sources.

Whether the decisions made at the time of the disappearance of Maclean and Burgess are considered to be right or wrong, it should be stressed that all Security Services are, for obvious reasons, correctly described as Secret. It is necessary for the government of the day to make sure that their activities can be justified, but one does not appoint a rat-catcher and then try to instruct him on how to catch rats. Perhaps, in deference to modern terminology, rats should be described as moles – a description of a special kind of spy with which the general public has only recently become familiar.

It would be ridiculous to argue that the head of any national security organization, whether the CIA, the KGB or MI6, is not far more autonomous than say the Chairman of British Rail. When it comes to making important decisions, however, the President of the United States of America or of the USSR or the Prime Minister of our own country have the ultimate deterrent should they consider those running the various Security Services to be a kakistocracy (rule by the wrong people). It is their prerogative to hire and fire.

MI5 is the British counter-espionage department whose main function is the tracking down of foreign agents in Britain. Their opposite number, MI6, is concerned with the collection of information about foreign governments. Their activities are usually the more arcane. 'Q' Section are the 'House Detectives' of the Foreign Office and, generally speaking, are more amateur than the real professionals. The Special Branch, usually rather deprecatingly referred to by the other branches as 'The Heavies', move in when it is considered that the time has come to intimidate or make an arrest.

In those pre-war days there was constant friction, not to say animosity, between our various Secret Services. During the pre-war period, MI5 considered communist infiltration to be of far greater importance than the pro-German movements. MI6 took a completely opposite view. This division of opinion caused a great deal of suspicion between the two Services at the time: today it is arguable that they were both right. Communism and fascism were equally dangerous.

The relationship between our own Secret Services and those of our allies, and in particular the Americans, has always been uneasy. The successes and failures of each are a matter for either recrimination or embarrassment. Each national organization tends to believe that only they are truly efficient and to be convinced that 'foreigners' have scant respect for secrecy. With this background, a clearer understanding is possible of the events which followed the news that, despite all previous denials, Burgess, Maclean and latterly Melinda and her family were indeed in Russia. ·

It may also make it easier to understand the inhibitions felt by successive governments over disclosing the true facts of Philby's ultimate defection twelve years later on the night of 23 January 1963 and the hysteria which stemmed from Margaret Thatcher's unexpected statement on 15 October 1979 that Sir Anthony Blunt had been known for some years past to have indulged in traitorous activities during the war.

To revert to Burgess and Maclean, it would have been the Special

Branch who were given the job of 'leaning' on Maclean, and I am reliably informed by someone who was a member of the Branch at that time that they had a man at Southampton standing by, if not to wave Maclean goodbye, at least to watch his departure.

There is no reason to suppose that this observer did not immediately telephone his superiors, inform them that Burgess had also boarded the boat and confirm its expected time of arrival at St Malo. From then on it would only have required a few more telephone calls to arrange for their journey to be tracked and their contacts observed without anyone from England following them. The Sûreté could have followed them to the Swiss border and handed them on to Swiss Intelligence. . . . The Special Branch would have had no reason then, or now, to publicize their knowledge of the defectors' escape route and contacts nor to divulge the help and co-operation they had had from foreign colleagues.

The fact that the pursuit of Maclean was, to put it mildly, un-enthusiastic, leads one to believe that evidence that he had finally decided to bolt induced a feeling of relief. The authorities would not, now, have to bring a shaky and potentially embarrassing case to court.

2 Assorted Adolescents

To understand what follows it is necessary to consider the climate of the 1930s. It was the decade during which Hitler rose to supreme power on the back of a new ideology. From the Japanese invasion of Manchuria in 1931 until the appeasers had to face facts in September 1939, the years had been punctuated by a succession of decisions and events which were more hotly (and, I am tempted to think, perhaps more intelligently) debated by the young pre-war generation of intellectuals than in the Houses of Parliament. There British legislators were going through one of the least inspired phases in their history.

That it was not only the young who were concerned by the events in Germany can be seen from a letter Lord Horder, then doctor to King George V, wrote to *The Times* in March 1933:

> Sir,
> The eyes of the civilized world are focused upon events that have been taking place in Germany since March 5 last. Amid the confusion of the various accounts that are presented from day to day one thing seems clear – that the effects of the counter-revolution must inevitably have their repercussions upon culture and upon thought in all countries.
> It is not my intention in this letter to express a view concerning the political implications, or the ethics, of recent developments in Germany, but there is one aspect which my conscience impels me to bring to the notice of your readers. I find it difficult to believe that, as has been reported, men and women of the highest attainments and standing in medi-

cine are being compelled to vacate their positions at the dictation of a prejudice that is narrow, racial, and, in this twentieth century, hardly conceivable. If report be true, the world is to be deprived, at the least for a time, of the humanitarian and scientific services of pre-eminent medical authorities in Germany on the ground that they are Jews.

We doctors are naturally dependent for any usefulness we may possess upon the labours of a brotherhood of medical science the world over; a brotherhood which knows neither race nor creed; and we needs must lose enormously by the sterilization of so fertile a source of knowledge as our German colleagues have for a very long time provided.

I would respectfully appeal to the learned medical societies of the country to keep in touch with the march of events in Germany, with a view, should the necessity arise – but I trust it may not – of registering in no ambiguous terms a sense of apprehension of the inevitable consequences of any action of this nature. Medical science can ill afford a sacrifice of so far-reaching a character.

     I am, Sir, yours faithfully,
       HORDER

These were the years, too, of hunger marches at home, of three million unemployed, of pathetic queues for the dole and the heady atmosphere of 'the intellectuals' war' in Spain, where some of the most brilliant young men of their generation lost their lives in an effort to give practical support to the ideas about which they were so articulate. There were many at the time who openly espoused the cause of communism, not particularly out of admiration for the Russian regime but as a protest against the rising cult of fascism.

Britain's counter-intelligence department, MI5, has had to put up with a great deal of criticism for not detecting those young communist idealists whose ideals hardened into active assistance to the Russians in later years. Although our pre-war Secret Services were not as efficient as they are today, being both short of funds and run on rather 'old-boy net' amateur lines, the criticism is not altogether justified.

It is important to remember that there were more dangerous forces at work at the time, which were considered to be a bigger threat to the country than the handful of largely intellectual and, in most cases, ineffectual communist sympathizers. The cult of fascism was far more real and far more pertinent. Sir Oswald Mosley's blackshirts openly strutted the streets wearing their swastika armbands. The windows of Jewish shops were smashed and giant rallies were held in places like the Earls Court Stadium, where Mosley's thugs cheered the fanatical rantings of their leader to the echo.

But there was a more arcane and more sinister side – fascist infiltration of the Establishment. Admiral Barry Domville for example ran an organization called 'Link', and was assiduous in his efforts to recruit prominent men in all walks of life. This was so successful that there is reason to believe that, had there been a German invasion, there would have been people in high places who would have come out in their true colours as Nazi supporters.

I was discussing this phenomenon recently with a highly intelligent member of the Establishment who, whilst up at Oxford before the war, found himself exposed to attempted brainwashing by fellow undergraduates, and even dons, who espoused the cause either of communism or fascism. In London he even attended secret meetings of the fascist underground where, he said, the views expressed and the plans laid for a British Anschluss were infinitely more dramatic than anything the communists could offer. The leader of that particular fascist cell, a highly esteemed art dealer, is still alive and his views are unaltered. Nor is he alone.

This then was the atmosphere when Burgess, Maclean, Philby and Blunt were all at Cambridge. It is interesting now, in view of later events, to consider their widely differing backgrounds in turn.

Because the name of Anthony Blunt has been paraded in the national Press and on television as a traitor and spy to a degree never achieved by Burgess, Maclean or even Philby it must not be assumed that this reflects his importance to the Russians. His notoriety stems from his connections with the Royal Household and the fact that, unlike the other three men, he was in England when his guilt was publicly revealed.

In many ways Blunt's motivation is easier to understand and even to sympathize with than that of any of the others. On the other hand his background during his formative years would, at first sight, have made him the least likely candidate for future conversion to Marxism and ultimately to employment as a communist agent.

Anthony Frederick Blunt was born on 26 September 1907, the younger son of a vicar. His father the Rev. A. S. V. Blunt was at the time the incumbent of a fashionable parish in Bournemouth. As was much more common at that time than it is now, he had adequate private means and a wide circle of influential friends. In those days for a churchman to have private means was almost as important as it was for an officer in a good regiment.

It was probably due to Blunt senior's social connections that in 1912 he was offered and accepted the post of Chaplain to the British Embassy in Paris. He was later to be awarded the OBE. It was certainly due to his financial stability that Anthony was able to follow his elder brother Wilfred to Marlborough, one of England's leading public schools.

Most of his boyhood before going to school and afterwards, during the holidays, was spent in Paris. There he had the opportunity of mixing in highly exclusive social circles. The British community in Paris centred upon the Embassy and the English Church, and there can have been few receptions given for important visitors to which the Reverend Blunt was not asked, and few private houses at which he and his family were not welcome guests.

It is probable that it was during these years that Anthony first met the young Duke of Kent, with whom he established a friendship which lasted until the Duke's tragic death in an air crash in 1942. There is evidence, too, that he was at least acquainted with many of the other young Royals, including the future Queen Mother.

Although there is no doubt that young Anthony enjoyed the social aspect of his boyhood in Paris, he early on developed an almost obsessive love of art – and what more fertile ground for this passion to flourish? Paris was at that time, if not still today, the cultural capital of Europe. He was also an exceptionally intelligent boy, as his scholastic record at Marlborough shows.

He spent his last holiday from Marlborough (before going up to Trinity College, Cambridge, in 1928) as tutor to the children of

René Gimpel, the owner of the Gimpel Gallery and an influential figure in the international art world. Gimpel was extremely impressed by the young tutor's precociously wide knowledge of art in general and his specialized knowledge of the works of the painter Poussin in particular. Poussin was to remain Blunt's favourite painter during his long and distinguished career as an art historian.

Blunt's years as an undergraduate confirmed his promise as an outstanding scholar without, at that stage, any tendency towards being distracted by the uncomfortable stirrings of political consciousness. Undoubtedly he had already discovered his predilection for homosexual relationships, but not to such a marked degree as to distinguish him from many of his fellow undergraduates. He took to the scholastic life like a duck to water, and luxuriated in the opportunity it gave him for serious study and intelligent conversation. Predictably he achieved high academic distinction and, in 1932, when he graduated with first class honours, he was offered and accepted a fellowship from his own college, Trinity, which he continued to hold until 1936.

Thus he was a near contemporary of Kim Philby, who had gone up to Trinity in October 1929 to read history. This was with a view to taking the Civil Service examination. Guy Burgess, who had gone up to the same college a year older than was normal, in 1930, was another contemporary. For some of the years when they overlapped at Cambridge, Blunt was a don whilst Burgess, Philby and Maclean (who alone went to a different college, Trinity Hall, where he read modern languages) were undergraduates.

I have no reason to doubt Blunt's own recent statement to the Press that his final conversion to Marxism took place in 1935 and that the person who converted him was Guy Burgess, then an undergraduate in his last year. It is certain that the two men were on terms of the closest friendship both personal and intellectual – although possibly their intellectual rapport was of greater importance.

During almost the whole of the preceding year, Anthony Blunt had been on a sabbatical during which he had spent part of his time in South Germany but had been mainly concerned with studying architecture in Rome. When he returned to his duties early in 1935 it was to find, he claims, that almost everybody in his closest circle of friends had espoused the teaching of Karl Marx.

Whereas the upbringing of Anthony Blunt was entirely conventional the same could not be said of Kim Philby, although in both cases their parentage might be loosely described as upper-class. Whereas the Rev. A. S. V. Blunt was very much a conformist, Kim's father, Harold St John Bridger Philby, was very definitely not. At the time of Kim's birth, St John Philby, as he later became generally known, had been for five years in the Indian Civil Service at a time when the British Raj was the very epitome of all the Empire stood for.

Not so very many years later, however, St John Philby started a lifelong love affair with Arabia, even to the extent of renaming himself Abdullah, which means 'slave of God'. He certainly could with some justice lay claim to being regarded as the leading Arabist of his time, but whether he was a genius or something less is still hotly debated amongst students of Arabic affairs. Certainly he was a colourful figure, and his influence on young Kim's life was a lasting one.

Kim was born, five years Anthony Blunt's junior, on New Year's Day, 1912. He was christened, rather pompously, Harold Adrian Russell, but almost from birth was known as Kim, after Rudyard Kipling's immortal hero.

It was a not inappropriate sobriquet. Much of his early childhood was spent squatting in the street outside the courthouse in Ambala in the Punjab waiting for his father to conclude his magisterial duties. His daily companions were Indian boys of his own age. Burnt by the sun to a deep brown, and speaking Tamil more fluently than he could speak English, he could easily have passed for one of them.

An interesting point in young Kim's early life is the seeming conflict between his father's increasing eccentricity, or at least anti-Establishment opinions, and his adherence to the conventional so far as his son's education was concerned. Although he himself spent more and more time in his travels through the Middle East and involved himself even more closely with Arab affairs, even to the point of being converted to the Muslim faith, he planned a completely conventional environment and upbringing for his family. He acquired a house in Acol Road on the outer periphery of Hampstead. Acol Road was the very epitome of middle-class respectability. The fact that many years later it was to become immortal amongst bridge players as the birth place of the Acol bidding system does nothing to detract from its almost oppressive suburbanism.

Whilst much has been written about the maverick St John, little has been mentioned about the influence of his long-suffering wife and the devoted mother of his children, Dora. She had all the stable, family-loving qualities which her husband so palpably lacked. It was Dora who held the whole family together, saw that they washed behind the ears and were sent tidily dressed to school each day. During his father's long absences, Kim Philby found himself in an entirely female household – his mother and his sisters, Helena, Patricia and Diana. It was a situation he enjoyed. Far from it resulting in a total rejection of women in favour of homosexuality it resulted in the pursuit of female conquests becoming one of his most abiding interests.

If further evidence were needed to demonstrate St John Philby's unpredictability it would be found in his insistence that his son follow in his own footsteps and be sent to Westminster School, one of England's oldest and most revered educational establishments. It is tucked in behind Westminster Abbey and cheek by jowl with the Mother of Parliaments. Westminster was so imbued with tradition and the necessity of maintaining old values that it was only in the year before Kim arrived there at the age of twelve as a King's Scholar that it had moved with the times sufficiently to approve the installation of electric light.

Westminster, with its preoccupation with the classics, its clinging to traditions handed down from generation to generation (to the extent of scholars being required to dress in the obligatory top hat and tails) and its allegiance to the time-honoured, and frequently painful, summary punishment for breaches of behaviour did not appear to sow the seeds of revolution in young Philby. On the contrary he is remembered as a slightly untidy youth, academically adequate if not outstanding like his father, and, with the achievement of prefectorial status, becoming less self-conscious about the stutter with which he had been afflicted since early childhood.

In all he appeared to be suitable material to follow his father into the Indian Civil Service, so that in the autumn term of 1929 he duly went up to Trinity College, Cambridge, to read history as a preparation for taking the Civil Service examination.

Guy Burgess's family were in rather more comfortable financial circumstances than either Philby, Blunt or Maclean. He was born in 1911 and from the first was an extremely difficult child – or as child psychiatrists would probably quite rightly claim, his development into adolescence was hampered by an adoring mother who gave in to his slightest whim. If thwarted he would lie on the floor and kick and scream until he got what he wanted. His father had been born in Aden into a family of long-standing military tradition. Malcolm Burgess broke with this tradition and joined the Navy, where he was not a great success. Whilst still a junior lieutenant he was severely admonished after an unfortunate collision at sea. He was luckier in love and in 1907 married an attractive daughter of wealthy parents, Evelyn Gillman. Guy Francis de Moncy Burgess was born the elder of two sons within sight of the Naval Dockyard at Devonport. During the 1914–18 war Guy saw little of his father, who was on active service. Malcolm Burgess was placed on the Retired List at his own request in 1922 and died of a horrifyingly spectacular heart attack in the presence of his family in 1924.

In spite of the fact that Burgess's father was, like Philby's, seldom at home and tyrannical when he was, when he died he induced in his son something of a father fixation. This probably switched to his mother after Evelyn Burgess remarried a retired American Army officer, Colonel John Retallack Basset. Basset made considerable efforts to be a good stepfather to Guy and his brother Nigel, and was generous in his financial support of Guy in his Cambridge days. Guy was unimpressed. It was Colonel Basset's innocent hobby to study racing form and bet in a modest way. When asked casually by an acquaintance about his father, Guy snapped: 'My own father died when I was thirteen years old. My stepfather, I am afraid, is a professional gambler.'

Malcolm Burgess was determined that Guy should follow him in the Navy, and entered his name for Dartmouth. However, at the time of his father's death Guy was too young to go there, and was sent off for a year to Eton. He left Eton on reaching the required age for Dartmouth: thirteen years and four months. A suggestion made by a journalist (and repeated by several others in later years) that he was sacked from Dartmouth for stealing is quite untrue. His eyesight was found to be defective and he was told that he was not eligible for executive duties in the Navy. It reflects some credit on Guy's year at Eton that his housemaster, Mr F. W. Dobbs, was able to arrange his re-entry. It was not an easy matter, and it was only because Dobbs was able to plead that he was a boy of outstanding ability that it was achieved.

The opinion of Robert Birley, later headmaster of Eton, given in 1928 shortly after Guy's return from Dartmouth, is also interesting. He taught Guy history and wrote:

> At the moment his ideas are running away with him, and he is finding in verbal quibbles and Chestertonian comparisons a rather unhealthy delight, but he is such a sane person, and so modest essentially that I do not feel this very much matters. The great thing is that he really thinks for himself. It is refreshing to find one who is really well read and who can become enthusiastic or have something to say about most things from Vermeer to Meredith. He is also a lively and amusing person, generous, I think, and very good natured. He should do very well.

Because of the Dartmouth interlude, Burgess was already a year older than most other freshmen by the time he went up to Cambridge in 1930. He was to read history, in which he had won an open scholarship to Trinity College.

The background of Donald Duart Maclean was as sharply contrasting as those of the three already described. His grandfather, John Maclean, came from the tiny island of Tiree in the Inner Hebrides. In order to escape, as so many Scottish islanders had done, from the grinding poverty of a community dependent on scraping a living from barren croft land, he came south to Lancashire, learned the trade of shoemaking and prospered modestly.

His son was to become first the Liberal MP for Bath and later possibly one of the least inspired Cabinet ministers of his time. He inherited all the dourness and narrow-mindedness of the 'Wee Frees'. Young Donald grew up in a deeply religious household where every morning started with family prayers, and where good living was regarded as the grossest form of self-indulgence. Alcohol in any form was, of course, completely banned. It must have come as a relief to Donald when his father decided, after much heart-searching, to send him to the relatively minor public school of Gresham's in Norfolk. Even there, however, he was not able to escape from his Calvinistic background entirely. The present headmaster of Gresham's describes the school credo then as 'a fanatical pursuit of purity' and says the pupils were not allowed to play games against other schools, 'in case the boys were contaminated'.

In spite of this restrictive atmosphere, it was at Gresham's that Donald Maclean was first able to develop intellectually and learn to survive amongst his fellows. One odd schoolfellow of his at Gresham's was the brilliant Jew James Klugman, whose father was also a prominent Liberal and Free-trader. Young Klugman went on to be a Fellow at Cambridge and a very active member of the Communist Party. It is possible, indeed probable, that Klugman was largely responsible for Donald Maclean's political development. In 1929 the tall, slim, almost good-looking Donald Maclean had no difficulty in passing into Trinity Hall, Cambridge, where he was to read modern languages with a view to a career in the Diplomatic Service. He went up in exactly the same term as Philby went up to Trinity. At Cambridge Philby joined the Labour Party. Burgess and Blunt tended, at this stage, to go underground, but Maclean seemed to protest his communist affiliations with openness and great vehemence.

His ambitions for a career in the Foreign Office appeared to be forgotten, although he continued to study assiduously and was ultimately to gain a very creditable degree. At the same time he was proclaiming to his harassed and bewildered mother, Lady Maclean, who had been widowed shortly after Donald went up to Cambridge, that he was a dedicated communist. As soon as he had got his degree, he insisted, he would be off to Russia to offer his services to the regime, probably as a teacher. In view of this it seems unlikely that Maclean had yet become an active Comintern agent.

Philby's political progress towards the extreme left was less marked, although that is not to say that he was not already aware in which direction his destiny lay. Of the four Philby was the least likely to hold purely intellectual convictions. As his subsequent career was to show, he had the greatest practical ability of all of them and the most overweening ambition. Perhaps his strongest motivation was a hunger for power, and perhaps it was only after he had left the university that he finally decided that the best way he could feed the hunger was by working for Russia.

By 1935 the Cambridge connection was over. Apart from the continued friendship of Burgess and Blunt, the four men's paths were to cross only intermittently in the years ahead. There were others among their contemporaries for whom the moment of political decision had come. Alan Nunn May chose the cloistered scholarship of the research laboratory and, in dramatic contrast, John Cornford rushed to join the International Brigade in the Spanish Civil War. He was killed on the day after his twenty-first birthday on 28 December 1936.

Whether Cornford or David Haden-Guest, who was also killed in Spain, would in the final analysis have agreed with a disillusioned Julian Bell is impossible to tell. Bell had written from Spain, where he was driving an ambulance, to C. Day Lewis: 'revolution is the opium of the intellectuals – pseudo-revolution.' For Bell at least it was to be his epitaph, for he too was killed shortly afterwards. What is certain is that those who had already become committed to what Kim Philby called his 'Silent War' were not having second thoughts.

Donald Maclean seems to have decided that he could play a more effective part in the silent war by joining the Establishment than by making grandiose gestures. After getting his degree he put all thoughts of going to Russia behind him, sat for the Foreign Office entrance examination and passed it comfortably.

That he had already set himself on a course of duplicity is demonstrated by his answer to a question put to him when he appeared before the Board of Examiners. He was asked: 'We understand,

Mr Maclean, that during your time at Cambridge you expressed certain communist sympathies. Do you still hold such sympathies?' It was a shock question, but Maclean was astute enough to realize that to deny the accusation would be fatal to his cause. Instead he said: 'I did indeed hold certain communist beliefs at that time. I have not yet *totally* rejected them.'

The Board, impressed by his apparent honesty, endorsed his application for establishment in the first grade of the Foreign Service.

3 The Cambridge Connection

I have already described the political climate at Cambridge during the 1930s, but of course it should not be imagined that Cambridge was the only university to be swept by conflicting ideologies, or that it was the only university where communism was fashionable amongst the more intellectual Dons and undergraduates.

The distinguished journalist Philip Toynbee, who was at Oxford at the same time, came, with many of his contemporaries, to believe in communism. Asked recently if at that time he would have been prepared to be an agent for the Comintern he replied with admirable honesty: 'I really don't know. Nobody asked me, but if they had it is quite possible that I would have agreed.' Since then A. J. P. Taylor has said that he was aware that, during his period as a lecturer in modern history at the University of Manchester, there were a number of communists amongst his students and that he was quite aware that Manchester was not an exception amongst the red-brick universities.

But it is the Cambridge communist group and four of them particularly whose activities have singled them out. When each of them first went up to Cambridge their political ideas had not crystallized, but in each of them, in their various ways, the seeds must already have been sown. Though Blunt was a Don he was on terms of the closest intellectual intimacy with many undergraduates. That this should be possible is one of the pleasantest aspects of English university life. His relationship with Burgess probably went beyond that. It also seems that the younger man dominated the older by the remarkable strength of his personality.

Because Burgess was almost a caricature of the extrovert and colourful undergraduates of his time, a rather fuller account of his Cambridge years may be of interest. His co-conspirators kept lower profiles.

Immediately after his arrival, Burgess became wholly and completely absorbed in all the more exotic aspects of university life. He joined the Pitt Club, the status symbol of the horsier and more conventional-minded undergraduates, but his extra-mural activities were soon to single him out as one of the most talked-about undergraduates of the time.

To begin with, he was what can only be described as a 'dedicated' homosexual. So much has been hinted at in relation to this subject about Burgess and Maclean that it is probably as well to put their 'deviationism' in perspective.

Burgess was entirely homosexual and made not the slightest attempt to conceal it. Rather he flaunted it, pursuing men with all the unabashed enthusiasm of a Piccadilly prostitute. Not only were his affairs legion, but he managed, by some strange power of personality, to keep his discarded lovers as friends long after he had lost interest in them sexually. Because of his brash, open approach he had a very considerable measure of success, far greater than the more inhibited homosexuals who try to satisfy their desires with the veiled approach and the carefully dropped hint.

Maclean was one of Guy Burgess's conquests, or so Burgess boasted to a mutual friend in later years. This does not militate against Tom Driberg's later report of Guy's reaction when asked whether he was having a homosexual relationship with Maclean in Moscow. 'Good God no!' Guy replied. 'Going to bed with Donald would be like going to bed with some great white *woman*.'

At the same time Maclean was not at all the sort of person one might expect to have homosexual tendencies. The two men could hardly have been less alike in temperament. Burgess, the brash, opinionated extrovert, ever ready with the apt epigram and devastating turn of phrase, contrasted oddly with the serious-minded and austere Maclean.

Maclean found it hard to shake off his Calvinistic upbringing. Realizing that he could never have the verbal agility of Burgess, he did not indulge in small talk and, unless he had had a lot to drink, rarely gave an opinion without appearing to give the matter a lot of thought. Yet according to those who knew him at the time he was very much under the influence of the volatile Burgess.

Although we do not know exactly when Burgess came into direct contact with an active agent of the Communist Party, it would seem at least likely that it was his loudly-voiced opposition to fascism which first brought him to the notice of the Comintern's recruiting officer. Several possible names, most of them Russian, have been put forward as candidates for this key post. At this stage it would be profitless to make any attempt at identification. Anyway, most of the people mentioned are now dead.

It was in his capacity as a member of the Anti-War Movement that Burgess took an extremely active part, for example, in an Armistice Day demonstration which can have done little to raise his stock with his fellow members of the Pitt Club. On this occasion Burgess and a group of fellow pacifists decided, as part of a general pacifist demonstration, to lay a wreath on the Cambridge War Memorial, inscribed 'In memory of the victims of an imperialist war which was not of their making'. The attempt was strongly resisted by another section of undergraduates and it was only as a result of the most warlike action that the pacifists were able to achieve their objective.

Burgess also managed to get himself involved, as many undergraduates have before and since, in well-meaning efforts to improve the lot of the college servants by urging them to corporate action – and with as little success. The subjects of his good intentions were the Hall waiters at Trinity, a section of the long-suffering but reasonably contented army of servants who, since time immemorial, have been the passing cause of the first stirrings of social conscience in successive generations of undergraduates. On this occasion matters got so far as the threatening of strike action, but history does not record how, this time, the college authorities dealt with the perennial situation.

Burgess joined in booing Neville Chamberlain, who was speaking as guest of honour at the Founder's Feast at Trinity, when the then Chancellor of the Exchequer claimed that although there were then two million unemployed, there was no real hardship being suffered by the men and their families.

But there must be few undergraduates who do not have a similar repertoire of youthful deeds of bravado, and these incidents hardly read like the early days of a devoted revolutionary. Perhaps his general attitude to these matters is most easily understood by the description of the part he played in the hunger marches of 1934 he gave to Tom Driberg in Moscow.

'In the Cambridge of those days,' Driberg wrote, 'socialist and communist undergraduates had many opportunities of demonstrating their opposition to the existing order. One was provided by the hunger march of 1934. With some undergraduates, Guy went to Huntingdon to meet the marchers, marched with them to Cambridge, and then went to London by train, to meet them again and march with them to Hyde Park.'

One cannot really feel that this leisurely, almost patronizing participation in one of the great tragedies of the time amounted to much more than a boyish lark calculated to enhance his reputation for left-wing intellectualism at the university, rather than to provide a real inspiration for the marchers. Certainly few present-day political demonstrators would expect to be taken very seriously on such low mileage.

Beneath this rather tiresomely naive exterior another side to the complex personality which was Guy Burgess was already beginning to take shape. There is no doubt that during his university career he showed signs of brilliance. He may well have fallen not far short of Goronwy Rees's description of him as 'the most brilliant undergraduate of his time'. Although in his third year he suffered a severe nervous breakdown, which resulted in his taking only an aegrotat degree, no less a personage than Dr G. M. Trevelyan urged both on Burgess and on Pembroke that he should become a Fellow of the College.

Cyril Connolly cites as further evidence of his brilliance that he was one of the half-dozen or so undergraduates invited to join that most select of all secret societies, the Society of the Apostles – a distinction he shared with his close friend Anthony Blunt, who may well have been responsible for his initiation. It is likely, however, that membership of this rather pretentious-sounding body, which has been in existence for over a hundred years, and prides itself on its sense of brotherhood and the 'utmost intimacy' into which its members at once fall, was a tribute to Guy Burgess's physical rather than his purely mental attributes.

Perhaps Guy Burgess's most striking characteristic was the quite remarkable personal influence he was able to exert on those who came into contact with him. It is true that he chose his friends, rather than was chosen by them, and that by far the majority of them were practising homosexuals, but this does not alter the fact that he was endowed with personal qualities of kindness and charm which enabled him to make friends easily.

It is also undoubtedly true that he used his talents in this direction quite shamelessly to achieve his own ends. To quote his own words, talking to Tom Driberg again, he exploited his advantages 'cynically and consciously'. Had it not been for this unusual degree of amorality, which, typically, Guy Burgess transformed into one of his most charming traits, it is quite likely that he would have been able to shed this communist phase, as did so many others, when he went down from the university. For most undergraduates it was an ephemeral experience which was not taken too seriously by the Communist Party itself.

Guy Burgess was, however, an unusual character and there is little doubt that he was recognized as such soon after he joined the Party. With his extrovert personality and his ability to influence people and his genuine intellectual interest in Marxism he was of much more potential value than the wishy-washy introverts who were usually attracted to the cause. It is true that he was never to play other than a minor role, but that is simply because there was nothing of real value, other than gossip and 'pillow-talk', that he was in a position to contribute.

It is typical of his nature that he was not only pathologically unable to keep anything which interested him to himself, but had a compulsion to influence other people with his own opinions and doctrines. It also made his importance as a serious spy minimal.

Whilst Burgess was strutting on the stage, Maclean, Philby and Blunt were playing less spectacular roles. All four were certainly part of the anti-war faction, but only Anthony Blunt has given an account of when and how he crossed the line between intellectual Marxism and becoming an active agent for the Comintern. In the course of the Press Conference which he gave on 21 November 1979, following his public unmasking by Mrs Thatcher, he gave the date as between 1935 and 1936.

During practically the whole of 1934 he had been on a sabbatical from his university duties. He had used this year for a comparatively brief stay in Southern Germany and then gone on to study architecture in Italy. He returned to Cambridge in October. At that time, and I now quote his exact words:

> I found that all my friends – that is an enormous amount of my friends and almost all the intelligent and bright young undergraduates who had come up to Cambridge – had suddenly become Marxists under the impact of Hitler coming to power and there was this very powerful group, very remarkable group, of Communist intellectuals in Cambridge of which Guy Burgess was one, James Klugman was another, John Cornford was another. It was a very remarkable group of enthusiasts, naive if you like, highly enthusiastic and highly intelligent and of those the person I knew best, whom I already knew very well was Guy Burgess. He had become a totally convinced Marxist and an open member of the Communist Party.

The final part of this statement is misleading. It may have been at this stage that Blunt himself was recruited by Burgess into becoming an 'active' member of the Communist Party, but this is a different matter from being an 'open' member. It may have been at this point that Blunt joined Burgess in agreeing to work for the Comintern, but the latter was already concealing his communism.

Blunt himself stayed on at Cambridge for another year before joining the staff of the Warburg Institute in London, in 1937, where he was to remain until the outbreak of war.

Philby, when he came down from Cambridge in the autumn of 1933, left almost immediately for Vienna. Austria had always seemed to him to be particularly interesting from a political point of view, and of course he was correct. It was no accident that Adolf Hitler's National Socialism was spawned in the heady political atmosphere of pre-war Vienna. Philby, already a dedicated Marxist, chose Vienna as a suitable centre to pursue some postgraduate studies in practical communism.

The *Sunday Times* team, Bruce Page, David Leitch and Philip Knightley, who wrote a biography of Philby published in 1968, claim that his lodging house-keeper's daughter Litzi not only inspired him to become actively involved in political affairs, but was also the first person he slept with.

Litzi's father was a Polish Jew called Israel Kohlman. His lodging house was a meeting place for Jewish intellectuals. They were deeply concerned with the anti-semitic holocaust which had already begun, and this probably served to harden Kim Philby's anti-fascist, intellectual Marxist beliefs to the point of persuading him to become actively involved in support of the Comintern. It does not seem likely, however, that Litzi gave him his first sexual experience. Philby had pursued women from an early age as assiduously as Burgess had pursued men. That he went through the whole of his university career primly preserving his virginity is unlikely in the extreme. Contrary to the current public view, homosexuality is not an essential qualification for being a spy. Philby was always a womanizer; Donald Maclean was, to all intents and purposes, bisexual.

The conclusion is irresistible that it was during Kim Philby's sexual and intellectual involvement in Vienna that he first became an active agent for the Soviet Union, and that he was recruited not by some shadowy figure lurking in the cloisters of a Cambridge college but probably by a Jewish and possibly a Russian member of the Comintern's Vienna network. In this he differs fundamentally from Blunt, Burgess and Maclean. Their positive decisions were made, whether for homosexual or ideological reasons, before they left Cambridge.

4 Postgraduates

After he had joined the staff of the Warburg Institute, which is largely concerned with postgraduate art studies, Anthony Blunt became indistinguishable from his fellow academics. He did not disguise his left-wing political views; neither did he actively propagate them. He is remembered by his pupils at that time as a courteous and helpful tutor much admired for his scholarship. He was to stay at the Warburg Institute until a few months before the war broke out in 1939. He then moved to the rival Courtauld Institute as Deputy Director.

Maclean played the part of the budding diplomat to perfection. He adopted the Foreign Office uniform of stiff collar, bowler hat and umbrella as evidence of his conformity and earned the regard of his seniors by his application and his very real ability. After two years in Whitehall he was posted as a Third Secretary to the British Embassy in Paris, where he was to meet his future wife Melinda and with her escape back to London just before the fall of France.

Philby married his Litzi, greatly to the displeasure of her parents and his, and returned with her to London. They settled in with the long-suffering Dora in the family home in Acol Road. Her new daughter-in-law confirmed all Dora's worst fears. She found her hard and bossy. To St John, then in Jidda, she wrote ominously: 'Just you wait till you see her.' She blamed Litzi for her son's extreme political views, with which she had no sympathy. 'I do hope he gets a job to get him off this bloody Communism,' she wrote. 'He's not quite extreme yet but may become so if he's got nothing to occupy his mind.' She had underestimated the strength of his political convictions. By this time he had become totally dedicated to the communist cause.

Philby's first thoughts were to follow his friend Maclean into the Foreign Office, and he filled in the application form which required him to supply the names of two referees as to character. One of the people he cited refused to recommend him as a suitable candidate, so the attempt was still-born.

He then turned his attention to his second choice, journalism, and managed with some difficulty to find a job with the *Review of Reviews*, then edited by Sir Roger Chance. There his immediate boss was Vernon Bartlett, later to become nationally known as a broadcaster and as Independent Member of Parliament for the Bridgewater Division in Somerset.

At this stage Philby appeared to take a sharp turn to the right politically, even to the extent of joining the expanding propaganda department of the Anglo-German Fellowship. Malcolm Muggeridge, who came to know Philby well and worked with him closely during the war in MI6, claims that this move was quite in character. Kim, he states, 'a born adventurer with very little political subtlety and always an eye to the main chance, was almost certainly attracted by the Anglo-German nonsense'.

In his own book, published some thirty years later, Philby writes of those times:

> During that period I was a sort of intelligence probationer. I still look back in wonder at the infinite patience shown by my seniors in the service, a patience matched only by their intelligent understanding. Week after week, we would meet in one or other of the remoter open spaces in London; week after week, I would reach the rendezvous empty handed and leave with a load of painstaking advice, admonition and encouragement. I was often despondent at my failure to achieve anything worthwhile, but the lessons went on and sank deep. . . .

In 1937 he took his first big step forward. He went to Spain and later got a job on *The Times* as a war correspondent. For his services to the right-wing cause against which so many of his erstwhile companions at Cambridge were fighting so bitterly, he was decorated by General Franco. The metamorphosis from the professed communism of his Vienna days to the right must have been thought by many to have been complete.

As may be expected, Guy Burgess's career after he left Cambridge was more colourful if less purposeful than that of any of the other three. After graduating he spent a postgraduate year at Cambridge during which time he turned down the possibility of an academic career by refusing the offer of a fellowship at Pembroke. His need was to get involved in something far more exciting.

It was during this year that he paid a visit to Russia. The trip arose out of discussions with his friend Goronwy Rees, a Fellow of All Souls, Oxford, who was one of Burgess's closest friends and one of the handful who were not homosexuals. Rees was also intensely interested in the practice and theory of communism, but in the end was unable to go with Burgess.

There are two views of the outcome of the trip. Rees holds the view that during the visit Burgess met many leading communists, including Nikolai Bukharin, and may well have been told how to play an active part as a Soviet spy. Burgess later hotly denied this, claiming that he did not meet Bukharin and that, even if he had, Bukharin had nothing to do with the Comintern.

Whatever the truth of the matter it was shortly after Burgess's return from Moscow that his friends noticed that his politics, like Philby's, had apparently changed. He started to claim that he had discovered some fundamental errors, not so much in the theory of communism as in its practice. He decided to quit the Party. This he did with all the rolling of drums and fanfare of trumpets which it is so easy to achieve inside the tightly knit circle of a university. Donald Maclean announced that he, too, had renounced communism at the same time. Burgess decided on a career in journalism and, as a true son of the Establishment, selected *The Times* for his debut. It was not a successful experiment and it only lasted for a month. Then he was back on the labour market, looking up his influential friends.

Victor (now Lord) Rothschild had known him at Cambridge so it was a natural enough move for Guy to ask himself down to stay at Victor's family house in the country. During this visit Burgess met Victor's mother, Mrs Charles Rothschild, who was enormously impressed by what her son had told her of his friend's political insight. After listening to Guy's own summing up of world affairs as they affected parts of the world in which the Rothschild family had financial interests, she was so impressed that she dispensed with the advice of the family banking house in the City and paid Guy Burgess a retainer of £100 a month to advise her on her personal investments.

That at least is the story which has gone down for the record, but it is one at which the imagination boggles. The picture of a young man supplanting the highly qualified financial advisers to one of the richest women in the world can only be accepted by the most gullible. It is much more likely that Burgess was recruited for a minor role in one of the Jewish Intelligence Services. It was a time when international Jewry, of which the Rothschilds were one of the leading families, was aghast at the anti-semitism then rampant in Germany. On Guy's many trips abroad during the years up to the outbreak of war his services as a messenger boy and intelligent observer of the scene could have been very useful. It was shortly after this that he made the first of many trips to Germany.

For a time after this Burgess took a job as personal secretary to Colonel Macnamara MP, who was, to put it mildly, extremely rightwing. In fact he was one of Admiral Barry Domville's converts to fascism. To friends who taxed Burgess with this seeming contradiction of everything in which he had expressed belief before, he would either make some vague remark to the effect that it was as well to understand every point of view, or go into a long diatribe purporting to explain that British Imperialist policy in India was the solution to world problems or some other equally unlikely thesis.

It was only some years after this that he gave Goronwy Rees what was the easiest explanation of this period in his life. They were sitting together in Burgess's flat near Ebury Street when he suddenly turned to Goronwy and said, with all the sincerity of the confessional box: 'I want to tell you that I am a Comintern agent and have been ever since I left Cambridge.'

Coming from anyone but Burgess, with his known love of the theatrical and compulsive desire to shock people, it would have been an odd statement. As it was, Goronwy, like many others afterwards, did not take the remark too seriously. Instead he asked, if this were so, why had he been so obviously right-wing in his thinking since he had left the university? 'Why not?' asked Burgess. 'Why else do you think I left the Party and left Cambridge and took that absurd job with that ridiculous MP? Did you really think I believed all that rigmarole about India and the Conservatives and the Nazis? But I had to invent something to say. The Party told me that I must break off all connection with them and as dramatically as possible, that I must quarrel with everyone I had known and try to start a political career of some kind. And I had to do it. So I did it. And all that nonsense served its purpose. Only I thought you were not taken in by it at the time. . . .' He then went on to suggest that Rees, too, should become an active worker for the Comintern. When Rees refused and expressed surprise that Guy had agreed to do so, he was informed that it was a step Anthony Blunt had also taken.

Goronwy Rees did not know quite what to do about this conversation. In the end he did nothing, and Burgess never mentioned the subject to him again. Only after Burgess had disappeared did Rees go to MI5 and repeat the revelations which he had found at the time too improbable to credit.

Burgess did not stay long with his Tory MP. Dr G. M. Trevelyan, who had given up trying to persuade him that he should adopt an academic career, interceded with Sir Cecil Graves, a high official in the BBC, with the result that after a short period of training Burgess found himself a member of the Talks Department.

Before long he had found a niche that suited him well. He was put in charge of a programme called 'The Week in Westminster'. His responsibility was to describe current affairs through the mouths of politicians of all parties in a week-by-week commentary on parliamentary proceedings. It was a job which gave him considerable scope for the exercise of his special talents. His ability to get on with people – and get things out of people – his quick grasp of the basic elements of a problem, and his general political awareness enabled him to turn what could quite easily have been a dull and boring programme into an extremely popular one.

It was also an interesting job from his own point of view in that it brought him into direct personal contact with a number of the leading political personalities of the day. Many of his most lasting friendships dated from this time.

Amongst other people whom he attempted to persuade to take part in the programme was Sir Winston Churchill, a man for whom he claimed to have great personal admiration. The interview took place at the time of the Czechoslovak fiasco and the signing of the Russo-German pact. Burgess travelled to Chartwell to see Churchill and, although circumstances prevented Churchill taking part in the programme, he was obviously impressed with the young man who came to see him. One of Burgess's most prized possessions from then on was a copy of *Arms and the Covenant* inscribed 'To Guy Burgess from Winston S. Churchill, to confirm his admirable sentiments. September 1938'.

'When the war comes, as we both know it will,' said Churchill (according to Burgess), as he gave him the book, 'I have no doubt they will send for me. Come and see me and bring this book to remind me. I will find you a useful job to do.' Burgess, when the time did indeed arrive, did not take him up on his offer. He was too busy in other directions.

Burgess's life in London during his BBC days was already beginning to assume the pattern which was, increasingly, to become his own. He was living in a small, comfortable flat which incorporated most of his ideas in interior design. It was decorated in red, white and blue, which, he claimed, was the only possible colour scheme one could ever live with, and the bedroom featured an enormous double bed with an Italianate bedhead. Indeed the bed in all his successive flats was of such proportions as to dominate the whole apartment.

Goronwy Rees who visited him in 1938 gives a fascinating glimpse of his way of life:

> How well I remember going round to his flat one fine sunny morning that summer. This morning the patriotic decor was completely submerged in the indescribable debris and confusion of the party which had evidently taken place the night before. He was in bed, in his blue sheets beneath his red counterpane, littered with the Sunday newspapers. Beside his

bed, on one side, stood a pile of books, which included *Middlemarch*, which he must have been reading for about the twentieth time, *Nicholas Nickleby*, Lady Gwendoline Cecil's *Life of Lord Salisbury*, Morley's *Gladstone* and Don Passos' *USA*. These were all favourite books of his, which he read and re-read, with the faculty of discovering something new in them at each re-reading.

On the other side of the bed stood two bottles of red wine and a very large, very heavy iron saucepan filled to the brim with a kind of thick grey gruel, a compound of porridge, kippers, bacon, garlic, onions and anything else that may have been lying about in his larder. This he had cooked the previous day, and on this he proposed to subsist to the following Monday. It contained, as he pointed out, everything which was necessary to sustain life, and what more could one require for intellectual happiness than the books which lay beside him on the other side?

And there for a blissful twenty-four hours he would lie, at intervals eating his gruel, dipping into his books and entertaining his cronies.

Among his friends at this time was the short, grossly obese Katz, who was said to have been with Bela Kun in Budapest and had just stopped being economic editor of the news agency Inprecorr. There was a mysterious Englishman who conducted some sort of export/import agency in the Balkans and hurried round to see Burgess whenever he was in England. There was the usual 'resident' boy who was a necessary concomitant to anywhere that Burgess lived. Like Oscar Wilde, Burgess preferred boys from the working class, whom he would have as house servants, bedfellows and chattels to lend to his friends. The current boy was typical, and was eventually passed on to his old friend Anthony Blunt and replaced from his seemingly inexhaustible source of supply.

Another friend was a peculiarly detestable Frenchman called Pfeiffer. Pfeiffer was tough, cynical and experienced in the ways of the world. He was also greedy for power, money and sex. It was this seedy character, who looked as if the height of his ambition might be to keep a male brothel, who suddenly became *chef de*

Cabinet to Daladier, then Prime Minister of France. And there was von Putlitz. In a way he was the oddest of them all. Like the rest of them he was a homosexual, but unlike most of them, he was a man of great culture and intellect. The von Putlitz family, of which he was the head, was one of the oldest and most powerful in Germany before the 1914 war. Leaving the management of his estates to his younger brother, he had entered the German Foreign Office. Burgess got to know him when he was appointed to a senior position under Ribbentrop in the German Embassy in London and he soon became one of his closest friends.

Whether Burgess had a hand in the matter or not will probably never be known, but the fact remains that one morning von Putlitz took a stroll across St James's Park from the German Embassy in Carlton House Terrace for a meeting with Sir Robert (later Lord) Vansittart, then Permanent Under Secretary at the Foreign Office. From that moment on von Putlitz joined the ranks of our spies. Dedicated to the destruction of the Hitler regime, he reported every move inside the German Embassy at the time when Hitler was plotting the destruction of Britain with Ribbentrop.

There is a sequel to the von Putlitz story which may well have had its origins in those smoke-laden, heavy-drinking evenings in Burgess's garish flat. After the war, after holding several minor jobs in Western Germany, von Putlitz once again took a short walk – this time from West Berlin to East. One of the few people to see von Putlitz after his defection was the writer and journalist Sefton Delmer, who died in 1979. To him he said: 'It may well be that my friend Guy Burgess was influenced in his decision to go to Moscow by my example.' When this was suggested to Burgess, he readily agreed, adding: 'I regard von Putlitz as one of the best and bravest men I have ever known.'

It is possible that Burgess's intense hatred of Nazism influenced von Putlitz to defect to the British side. Certainly he knew von Putlitz was working for the British and von Putlitz probably knew of Burgess's communist affiliations.

Another episode from this period does not show Burgess in such a good light. It concerns the distasteful Pfeiffer.

Burgess was still 'advising' Mrs Rothschild and, in the course of his work for her, paid a number of visits to Paris. This was at the time of the Czechoslovak crisis, and Pfeiffer enlisted his aid to be a personal emissary between Daladier and Chamberlain. Although the letters were signed by subordinates, it provided for a time a completely unofficial channel of communication between the two premiers at a time when a complete understanding of each other's views, both official and unofficial, was of the utmost importance.

Guy performed his role with his usual punctiliousness, omitting only to inform Pfeiffer (and of course the two principals involved) that he was having all the letters photostated before delivering them. This he had done by a man he used to meet at the St Ermin's Hotel in Westminster, at that time a sort of Stock Exchange in the spy world.

These copies Burgess claims he passed on to an unofficial intelligence organization, adding that the only knowledge he had of their contents was when he was asked by the recipient to help him with translating them, as his own French was not very good. What he remembers of them he describes as 'the communications of a panic-stricken patriot to an ignorant provincial ironmonger' – a typical example of the sort of meaningless generalizations with which he used to amuse and impress his friends.

The end of this affair, if Burgess's account of it is to be believed, is very odd indeed. At a vital stage in the proceedings Pfeiffer called Burgess to Paris to collect another communication. On this occasion, however, he seems not only to have known of the contents of the letter before delivering it to be photographed, but to have disapproved of them. As Driberg put it in his book:

> The letter insisted that Daladier was violently opposed to the Fleet mobilization. But Guy had other information which indicated that this was not in fact Daladier's own view, and that he had been forced by Bonnet and others of the Right to adopt it as part of an internal cabinet manoeuvre. Guy, therefore, suppressed the letter.

At about the time of this peculiar incident, Henlein, the Czechoslovak Quisling, was on a visit to London and happened to stay at an hotel where one of Burgess's young friends was working as a telephonist. Burgess arranged for this youth to make notes of all the notes made by Henlein and passed the information on to MI5.

These examples of Burgess's activities are very revealing of his nature. His curiosity was all-consuming and completely catholic. Like a jackdaw, he had a compulsion to acquire anything that glittered irrespective of its value. The information which he obtained about Henlein's telephone calls can hardly have been of world-shaking importance, nor was it information which MI5 themselves could not have arranged to get had they thought it sufficiently worthwhile. Nonetheless Burgess could not resist taking advantage of the coincidence of having influence with his telephone operator boyfriend to get in on the act.

All these incidents add up to little more than playing at boy scouts. Is there any evidence that Burgess was playing a deeper game? There is one odd incident which seemed innocent enough to those who witnessed it at the time, but to which later events gave a sinister twist.

One Sunday morning Burgess rang a married couple and suggested meeting for lunch. 'I have got a personal letter to deliver in the East End. Let's have lunch at a Chinese restaurant,' he suggested, naming a well-known East End restaurant which they had visited on many occasions. When they arrived, Burgess excused himself for a moment and, crossing the road, put a letter through the box of a closed shop selling seamen's equipment and second-hand clothing.

Knowing Burgess's reputation for having bizarre friendships, nobody thought anything of the incident until after his disappearance. Then, anyone who had had the slightest association with Burgess was cross-questioned closely, and his lunch companions were no exception. They told the story of the letter, and, rather to their surprise, MI5 men drove them to the area and asked them to point out the shop where the incident took place.

By sheer chance – for it had all happened many years before, and the couple had not been back since – they were able to identify it. The Intelligence officers nodded in satisfaction. 'We have known for a long time that that was a "post office" for Soviet agents,' they said.

Here, then, is the first indication that has come to light that Burgess may actually have used the facilities of the Soviet spy network, though for what purposes and to what extent are unknown. His letter may have had an innocent explanation – perhaps he was writing to a sailor friend – or it may not.

That he was capable of treachery is undoubted. His particular brand of amorality, combined with his intellectual conceit, enabled him to regard any information which came into his possession as his own personal property to do with as he wished. If, as in the Pfeiffer instance, he decided that a document should be suppressed it would present no insuperable moral hurdle. If, in his infinite wisdom, he decided that the information would be of value to whichever cause he was espousing at the time, equally he would not hesitate to send it to them.

In attempts to prove that Burgess was a deliberate single-minded spy, much has been made of the fact that he was often seen to have large sums of money on him, or that he left rolls of notes lying carelessly about his flat. It would be extremely dangerous to draw conclusions either way from this evidence. The money might have been received from perfectly legitimate sources. Mrs Rothschild, for example, may have preferred to pay for his services in cash, and it is certain that at this stage MI5 did.

In the last years before the war Burgess did pass on information to MI5, particularly on Germany, and was paid for it. He was not regularly employed by MI5 but worked for them as a freelance.

Mr Selwyn Lloyd, explaining this rather extraordinary position in the House of Commons soon after Burgess and Maclean had departed, claimed that Burgess had only been recompensed for his efforts with expenses. All payments made by MI5 in these circumstances are, for obvious reasons, described as 'expenses'. Payments, too, are invariably made in cash. Any other form of payment might well tax even the ingenuity of a Burgess to explain, if hauled before the Commissioner of Inland Revenue. So the sums of money which Burgess left lying about are capable of a variety of explanations.

In December 1938, Guy Burgess decided to resign from the BBC. On the face of it, it was a strange decision. He was doing extremely well in his job. He was satisfying his urge to make friends and influence people and, to a degree, he had influence himself. His reason was that he had been offered an undercover job which had much greater appeal for him.

In the summer of 1939, whilst everyone was holding their breath and the outbreak of war was becoming more and more inevitable, Burgess met a very odd character indeed, called Colonel Laurence Douglas Grand, a regular soldier in the Royal Engineers. At the time that Burgess met Grand, however, the latter had just been detailed by the War Office to set up a new section whose role would have delighted the heart of a fictional spy writer.

It was known as Section D (the D stood for destruction), and its object was to train both propagandists and saboteurs to create havoc behind the enemy lines on the pattern of the Spanish Fifth Column. One of Burgess's MI5 contacts had recommended him to Colonel Grand, and without further ado this caricature of a gentleman spy offered Guy a job. Needless to say Guy immediately resigned from the BBC and set to work with the utmost enthusiasm.

Shortly after this Burgess arranged to meet Philby, reluctantly pinned down in St Jean de Luz recording the death throes of the Spanish Civil War. Philby was still in a mood of extreme frustration that his employment did not allow him to be as active as he would have liked in the interests of his Soviet spymasters. He must have listened with envy to his friend's typically colourful account of the surprising turn his career had taken.

5 The War

The expected outbreak of war on 3 September 1939 immediately resulted in a change of course for Blunt, Philby, Burgess and Maclean.

The air-raid sirens which had sounded on the first day of war in London proved to be a false alarm. The 'phoney war', during which no shots were exchanged, lasted into 1940 and Donald Maclean remained *en poste* in Paris.

Donald met his future wife in the Café de Flore, one of the more bohemian bistros which he liked to frequent as a relief from the respectable image he was at such pains to present as a member of the British Embassy staff. They had been introduced by a young English friend of Maclean's, Mark Culme-Seymour, and an American writer, Robert McAlmon.

Melinda Marling came from a middle-class American family who were rich and getting richer. Her parents had separated and her mother, who later became Mrs Dunbar, took her daughters, Harriet, Catherine and Melinda to Switzerland for a European finishing school education. Melinda in particular had overreacted to her exposure to European culture. When she met Donald she was going through a phase of intellectual bohemianism, smoking large Havana cigars and giving her left-wing views on world affairs with a glass of absinthe in her hand until far into the night. The attraction between Melinda and Donald was mutual but it was only when Hitler launched his Blitzkrieg in May 1940 and breached the Maginot Line that Maclean asked her to marry him.

They were married on 10 June in Paris, with the sound of enemy gunfire already audible in the distance. They joined the mass migration from Paris and got as far as Chartres after the first day, struggling down a road choked with refugees. Thus their bridal night was spent under a hedge in a rather damp field. Thirteen days later they sailed for England from Bordeaux in a British destroyer which, after ten days of zigzagging to avoid enemy submarines, eventually got them home safely.

Maclean stayed on in wartime London for the next four years. Melinda, expecting their first baby in 1941, sailed to America for the birth, but the child was stillborn and she flew sadly back to be with her husband, despite the Nazi bombs then tearing London apart. They were bombed out of two flats and once they were nearly killed in an air raid. But Melinda stuck it out, spending her days working in The Times Book Shop. When the air-raid sirens wailed, she refused to take cover in a shelter. She had tried it once and hated it. 'I'd rather die in bed than face it again,' she said.

But worse than the bombs, for Melinda, were the constant rows they were having, sparked off by Donald's drinking and fanned by her own fiery temper. He would go on for quite long periods as a purely social drinker and then break out on a spree of mammoth proportions when he would become argumentative, sometimes violent and often indiscreet.

These drinking bouts had worried Melinda even before she married him. Whilst on a short holiday in the South of France she wrote to him: 'If you do feel an urge to have a drinking bout why don't you have it at home? At least you will be able to get safely to bed.'

The fears which she had so impetuously brushed aside in those last unreal days before the fall of France were being realized. Although they still had times of almost idyllic happiness they were fewer and further between.

By this time, Philby was also back in England having been to France as a war reporter, still working for *The Times*. On 10 June 1940, the day on which Donald had married Melinda, he received an unexpected telegram from the War Office. The result was that he went immediately to keep an appointment with a middle-aged spinster called Marjorie Maxse. The place was the foyer of the St Ermin's Hotel in Caxton Street, where a few years before Guy

Burgess had been wont to meet some of the more mysterious of his acquaintances.

At that first meeting Kim was closely questioned by the almost intimidatingly formidable Miss Maxse and then ordered to keep another appointment with her at the same place and the same time a few days later. To his surprise Miss Maxse was this time accompanied by Guy Burgess. Here is Philby's own account of the second meeting from his autobiography, *My Silent War*:

> I was put through my paces again. Encouraged by Guy's presence I began to show off, name-dropping shamelessly as one does at interviews. From time to time my interlocutors exchanged glances; Guy would nod gravely and approvingly. It turned out that I was wasting my time as a decision had already been taken. Before we parted, Miss Maxse informed me that, if I agreed, I should sever my connection with *The Times* and report for duty to Guy Burgess at an address in Caxton Street, in the same block as the St Ermin's Hotel. . . . I decided that it was my duty to profit from the experience of the only secret service man of my acquaintance. So I spent the weekend drinking with Guy Burgess. On the following Monday, I reported to him formally. We both had slight headaches.

He claims that he had no idea who Marjorie Maxse might be. It is a point on which I can enlighten him. At the time of their meeting and almost up to the end of the war she was the Director of the Children's Overseas Reception Board and Vice-Chairman of the WVS. By the end of the war she had become Vice-Chairman of the Conservative Party, and on her retirement she was made a Dame of the British Empire. It all goes to show that you can never be sure of who anybody is. The job to which Miss Maxse had recruited Philby was of course in Colonel Grand's Section D, which had just been granted a very large budget in order to expand their operations.

Within a year Operation Grand had sunk without a trace, and those of its members who had not been fired became the nucleus of SOE. Colonel Grand himself, after being relieved of the leadership of his intrepid band of saboteurs, was promoted to the rank of Major General and put in charge of Fortifications and Works.

Anthony Blunt's baptism of fire at the outbreak of war was tinged with much the same sort of near comedy, which never seems to me to be very far beneath the surface when reviewing his own record and those of the others with whom his name has suddenly become so closely associated in the public mind.

It should be remembered that at the outbreak of war the first panic was to discover men of specialist talent in civilian life and utilize their services in the war effort, where they could be most useful. For example, when one of the Glucksteins of Salmon and Gluckstein, who owned the vast catering organization of J. Lyons, enlisted, he was eagerly seized upon and at once promoted from the rank of second lieutenant of a few days' standing, to that of brigadier in the Army Catering Corps. This was an eminently sensible use of specialist skill, but I can remember his telling me with some amusement that when he went to Gieves the military tailors and asked them to transform the insignia of a one-pip lieutenant to the red-tabbed magnificence of a brigadier, they would not allow him out of their shop until they had telephoned the War Office to confirm that he was not some sort of an impostor.

In the same way it was perfectly natural that in looking for recruits for the Intelligence Corps the powers that be should scan the lists of University Dons, and that the name of Anthony Blunt should automatically recommend itself to them. The result was that Blunt was instantaneously recruited into the Intelligence Corps and sent to the Training Headquarters at Minley Manor.

It is perhaps comforting to know that forty-eight hours later the Commandant at Minley was informed that Blunt's name had been withdrawn from the course because his communist sympathies had become known. At least some sort of rough and ready screening process was in operation then.

The sequel is not so comforting. He was immediately promoted to the rank of captain and sent to Europe in command of a section of twelve men with responsibility for field security. As a result, a rather surprised and nervous Anthony Blunt found himself in

Northern France as the German Panzer divisions raced to trap the British Expeditionary Force. I am indebted to one of the men who served under him at that time, Mr George Curry, now Secretary of the Board of Trustees at the University of South Carolina, for a description of Blunt at that time. 'I remember him well,' says Mr Curry. 'He was very tall, pencil-thin, with a mop of brown curly hair and a great deal of languid charm. But he was a hopeless officer.'

Blunt's section had gone to France in the month following the outbreak of war, October 1939. They were made up of young linguists with a vague sort of spy chasing role. Captain Blunt and his section had their headquarters in Boulogne, where their role was to cover the Northern sector up to the Belgian border.

What would Captain Blunt's feelings have been at this stage? At that time the Soviet Union had signed a pact with Germany which was to last until the summer of 1941 – thus, active communist supporters like Anthony Blunt and the rest might well have been excused for feeling that their communist sympathies and their abhorrence of fascism had been hopelessly compromised. By some sort of Orwellian double-think however, it would now appear that this was not the case with Captain Blunt.

However he may have reconciled his political allegiances at that time, on 24 May Blunt was faced with the necessity of taking practical steps to save his own skin. On that day, he found his section in Boulogne completely surrounded and cut off, with the only possible escape route back across the Channel. To add to his troubles, even in the unlikely event of his deciding to make a stand to the last man and the last round, his section had no arms except Blunt's obligatory revolver with five bullets. Again I quote Mr Curry:

> Blunt seemed to be completely indifferent. In fact, it was only when we got a call from someone in the Navy back in Dover telling us to get out fast that we decided to do so. And then we had to go and dig Blunt out of his billet in the town.
>
> We got away – six of us – with him in a small ship that had been sent in with munitions to blow up what it could of the harbour. That ship didn't have time to unload before we got

away. The other six chaps tried to get out through Dunkirk and we lost them.

It was hardly an operation which could have won Blunt any medals.

Nothing much need be said about the roles of our Four Musketeers between the phoney war and the end of hostilities in 1945.

After the collapse of Colonel Grand's Section D, Philby found himself – somewhat to his surprise, but no doubt to his satisfaction – recruited as a member of SOE. Late in 1940, both Burgess and Philby reported to the headquarters of this comparatively new organization at 64 Baker Street.

Shortly afterwards, Guy Burgess was sent for by Colin (later Major General Sir Colin) Gubbins, the new and immensely efficient Training Director of SOE, and fired without any explanation being given. His anguish at this unexpected setback to his espionage career can be imagined. Philby, his one-time protégé, on the other hand went on to greater things.

Burgess returned with his tail between his legs to the BBC, where ironically he found himself running a sort of Lonely Hearts programme called 'Can I Help You?'

Anthony Blunt, after his brief if somewhat disastrous involvement with the realities of war, returned to London and, almost at once, was recruited into MI5, the section of the Secret Service involved in counter-espionage. When asked recently how he managed to get accepted by MI5 he replied that it was on the recommendation of a friend who was already a member. This would undoubtedly have been the case. He has refused to divulge the name of his sponsor, but it might have been someone like Victor Rothschild, who had been an early recruit.

Anthony Blunt continued to keep in close contact with friends and with fellow communists from his Cambridge days and elsewhere. Hugh Thomas in his biography of John Strachey has recorded an interesting example. John Strachey was, of course, well known before the war for his impassioned pro-communist propaganda. His wealthy upper-class background gave him particular notoriety. To quote Hugh Thomas:

For a time Strachey stayed with Celia's [his wife's] mother who had always liked him and later, briefly, at the house of Lord Rothschild, 5 Bentinck Street, with among others, Guy Burgess and Anthony Blunt. . . . With Burgess he had endless political discussions, though Burgess's espionage was concealed from him; nor did he join Burgess on his wild raids through the blackout of war-time London, in the company of Brian Howard, in search of delectable youth.

Rothschild had lent his Bentinck Street flat for the duration for the use of his friends, and for a time both Burgess and Blunt used it freely.

Brian Howard like Burgess was an old Etonian and a homosexual. He had gone up to Oxford in 1922 and spent most of his postgraduate career mincing around on the fringes of society in London. He had tried desperately hard to get into MI5, but he proved too much even for them at a time when they badly needed recruits. Howard spent most of the war as a uniformed clerk in the Air Force.

Hugh Thomas's words are also interesting because of Blunt's recent statement that he talked to Burgess about everything under the sun except politics. Burgess's main topic of conversation was politics and it is unlikely, to say the least, that Blunt did not join in the discussions with Strachey as well as on other occasions.

Blunt stayed with MI5 up to the end of the war, during which time he conscientiously retailed any piece of information which might be even remotely useful to his Russian contact. His job, certainly for the first years of the war, was, however, of such unimportance that there can have been few secrets of real value for him to betray. He himself says that the extent of his spy activities at first was to give the names of colleagues and routine office matters, and there is no reason to doubt him. In the final year of the war he had a rather more senior position, but it was largely concerned with German intelligence, and again he had only minimal access to reports on the activities of British intelligence sources.

Philby's war was rather more interesting. After he had sacked Burgess, Colin Gubbins sent for Philby and asked him to produce a syllabus for the training of recruits in the techniques of underground propaganda. The school was set up on Lord Montagu's estate on the Beaulieu river and the students were all sorts of strange fish of almost every European nationality – including one German. The British contingent consisted of such widely diverse personalities as Paul Dehn, the distinguished writer and poet, Hardy Amies, the dress designer, and John Wedgwood of the pottery family.

Another appointment of near genius was that of Tómas and Hilda Harris to look after the catering. Tommy Harris and his wife were as much famed in pre-war London for their lavish hospitality at their house in Chesterfield Gardens as they were for the art gallery specializing particularly in Spanish art which they ran from their home. Both of them were brilliant cooks, and when shortly afterwards Philby's next appointment took him to London, the Chesterfield Gardens house became as much a convivial meeting place for Philby's 'Gang' as did 5 Bentinck Street for Blunt and others who took advantage of Lord Rothschild's hospitality. (Apart from Burgess and Blunt the latter included people like Louis MacNeice, the poet, Richard Llewellyn-Davies, and Theresa Mayor, who was later to become Victor Rothschild's second wife.) By now Kim had divorced Litzi. For him and his new wife Aileen, Chesterfield Gardens became a home from home and provided an opportunity for him to keep in touch with many of his old Cambridge associates.

In 1941 Philby was transferred from SOE to a new job with Section V of MI6. He was concerned with Britain's increasing efforts to infiltrate German security in the Iberian peninsula. It was a job at which he was extremely good, and he was quickly recognized as one of the leading experts in the field. North Africa and Italy had soon been added to his parish.

In 1942 Section V moved from bomb-scarred London to the comparative safety of St Albans, but Kim did not long have to endure a Spartan existence, deprived of the Harris' hospitality. By 1943 he was back in London.

In 1944 he was transferred yet again to take over the immensely important Section IX, which was being set up not to operate against Germany but against international communism and the Soviet Union. At this stage he became of absolutely vital importance to the Russians. His value to the KGB may be judged in the light of the Volkov case, which set all his nerve ends jangling.

Very briefly, Konstantin Volkov, a Vice-Consul in the Soviet Consulate in Istanbul, had asked the British Consul for political asylum in Britain. He declared that he was in fact an officer of the KGB, and that in return for asylum he would divulge, amongst other things, the names of three senior Soviet agents then working in Britain. This information arrived one morning on Philby's desk, and he immediately realized that he was one of the agents to be named. Fortunately, in giving Philby this information, his immediate chief, Page, insisted because of its extreme importance that Philby handle the matter personally.

In the event it was decided that Philby should fly to Istanbul to have a meeting with Volkov in the presence of John Reed, the First Secretary at the Embassy. Space does not permit of a detailed account of this immensely exciting incident, but anyone who is interested can read about it in detail in Philby's autobiography.

In the event, by the time Philby had arrived in Istanbul, Volkov had disappeared. The Russians had claimed their own and he was never heard of again. Philby's final lines in the chapter he devotes to this matter read: 'Another theory – that the Russians had been tipped off about Volkov's approach to the British – had no solid evidence to support it. It was not worth including in my report.'

It is impossible not to conclude that Philby himself was the only person who could have supplied that solid evidence.

6 The Cold War

To continue in a dull job was not a situation that Guy Burgess's ego would allow him to tolerate for long, and he made constant efforts to get out of the BBC and into something more to his taste. It was not, however, until June 1944 that, by devious string-pulling, he managed to get himself transferred from the safe haven he had joined in 1940 to the dubious status of temporary civil servant in the Foreign Office News Department. It turned out to be an inspired move. Whilst he was there he took the Foreign Office competitive examination and succeeded in getting himself established as a member of the permanent staff.

Shortly after this triumph he was at his desk in the News Room, engaged on some routine task, when the telephone rang. At the other end was Hector McNeil, Labour Member of Parliament for Greenock. He was a remarkable man. Although a Glaswegian from a very poor family, he had managed to get himself a respectable education and then fought his way up the journalistic ladder. He was a promising employee of the Express group when he resigned to stand for Parliament. Though his accent betrayed his origins, he was well read, well informed and a lively and entertaining companion in any company. His wits were quick, his sense of humour excellent, his energy phenomenal. He was a glutton for work but played hard in the few hours of relaxation he allowed himself. He saw all too little of his wife and family, to whom he was devoted, because of official engagements and travels abroad. He spent occasional evenings off equally at ease with raffish companions from his Fleet Street days at El Vino's and in modest Soho restaurants or playing excellent bridge after a formal dinner party with smart society friends. I have yet to meet a Foreign Office official who knew him in those days who did not express both respect and affection for him. Tragically, he died in 1955.

Guy had met him in the old 'Week in Westminster' days and had maintained contact ever since. McNeil had just been appointed to the Labour government with the job of Minister of State at the Foreign Office, and he wanted Burgess to be his Personal Assistant. At last Guy Burgess, known to a wide circle of friends as a homosexual, near-alcoholic and communist sympathizer, was very near indeed to the seat of power.

So far little has been said about Burgess's drinking habits. It is, however, an important aspect in any appraisal of the man. He was a heavy drinker from his earliest Cambridge days. Derek Blaikie, on his return from their trip to Moscow, used to regale his Oxford colleagues with the story of losing Burgess and finding him, eventually, dead drunk in the Park of Rest and Culture. It was only after he started to live in London, however, that his drinking assumed the proportions of a 'compulsion'. His favourite day-to-day drink was red wine, which he consumed in copious quantities, but it was when the whisky bottle came out that the trouble really began. Sir Harold Nicolson, whose admiration for Burgess survived his flight to Moscow – although he disapproved of his bitten and dirty fingernails – remarked on the brilliance and colourfulness of his personality until he had had too many drinks. Then, he said, he became boring and incoherent.

A fascinating cameo of life as it was lived in Hector McNeil's outer office is given by Goronwy Rees, who called in to pick up a book which Burgess had promised to lend him. The book was *The Kinsey Report on the Sexual Behaviour of the Human Male*, which had not yet been published in this country but of which Burgess had had a special copy sent from America. There had, he explained, been such a queue of Foreign Office officials who wanted to borrow it that he had had to lock it away in a safe place.

'I'll have to go and get it,' he said. 'You had better come with me.'

I quote here, verbatim, the story as Goronwy Rees told it to me in 1962:

I followed him down the broad corridors of the Foreign Office until we came to what was evidently a very important room indeed. Even Guy stood for a moment abashed on the threshold.

'It's all right,' he said, 'he's not in,' and pushing open the door, entered a vast room which seemed to be all red plush and rather heavy, brocaded curtains. A table ran the whole length of the room, and in the middle of it, with its back to the long windows, was a heavily and ornately carved chair.

'It's the Foreign Secretary's room,' explained Guy airily. 'I thought you'd like to see it. I love it.'

In one corner of the room was an open safe, which had obviously long ceased to have any use for security purposes, as its doors stood open and the shelves within seemed to be filled with reference books. Guy fumbled among them for a moment then withdrew his hand holding the Kinsey Report.

'I keep it here,' he explained. 'I know no one would think of looking for it and, if Ernie found it, he would not know what it was – and even if he did he would not want to read it.'

Rees gave a slightly different version of this story to Andrew Boyle, but before reading his book I had already decided that mine needed modification. Barley Alison, who was in the Foreign Office at the time and knew Burgess quite well, laughed when she read it and said, 'I know the room where he kept his copy of the Kinsey Report. It was certainly not Ernest Bevin's office. It was one of the conference rooms which was available to anyone for committee meetings or discussions with visitors.'

Indeed it was rather like a studio at the BBC which Programme Controllers could book. To the outside observer it might look like a room of great importance but it was not. Guy was, as usual, indulging in a little bit of typical self aggrandizement.

Most of this account of Guy Burgess's life while he was in the Foreign Office is quoted from the book Purdy and I wrote in 1963. One of the difficulties we encountered at that time was the sensitivity of officials who had been closely involved at some stage of their careers with either Burgess or Maclean. Whilst we were allowed to call his colleague in Hector McNeil's office 'Fred', we were not allowed to give his full name. We were advised that this might result in a suit for libel.

Fred Warner was a close colleague rather than a particular friend of Burgess's. He subsequently went on to become one of our most brilliant diplomats, finally serving as British Ambassador in Tokyo, where he and his wife Simone were extremely popular and he earned a well-deserved knighthood. He was recently elected to the European Parliament. It was certainly an official, rather than his personal decision, that his name should be disguised. He himself was abroad at the time.

Whilst I sometimes find security restrictions tiresome and inhibiting, I do not regard them as draconian. In this instance, however, the removal of Warner's name was tiresome and silly, if only because it caused my co-author and me to suspect some sinister cover-up and waste much valuable time trying to fit him for the role of Third or Fourth Man. I am now satisfied that our suspicions were utterly groundless, but too much official sensitivity does nothing but increase, rather than diminish, suspicion about the individuals concerned. Many were then suspected unjustly when their involvement in the tangled web of loyalty or disloyalty was entirely professional and innocent.

If Burgess was never reprimanded for his drinking habits at the Foreign Office, he was the subject of at least one critical inter-office memo which, like so much in his life, had all the overtones of high comedy. It read in its entire simplicity: 'Mr Burgess will, in future, refrain from munching garlic during office hours.' This sprang from his deplorable habit of using garlic, not as a flavouring but as a vegetable – a vegetable, moreover, which he carried around in his pockets, kept in the drawers of his desk and munched continuously to the distress and alarm of everyone around him.

Apart from lunchtime sessions, which usually took place at the Reform Club, his drinking bouts, when they were not in his own or somebody else's flat, usually took place in Soho. One of his favourite haunts was an afternoon and evening drinking club called the Mandrake, which had its being in a backstreet basement off Dean Street. This was in those days a very offbeat club, frequented by an extraordinary mixture of artists, writers, poets and hangers-on who seemed to have little to do all day but sit around drinking and playing endless games of chess. Burgess was a member of long standing, paying his guinea a year membership by banker's order – unlike Maclean, who also used the club but never paid his subscription.

As the then proprietor, Boris Watson, told me: 'I often used to find Maclean there when I came down, either drinking by himself or with other friends who were not members. I chucked him out time and again, but he always used to try and get in again, usually when he was drunk.' He was never, however, so far as anyone can remember, seen drinking with Burgess.

Another favourite drinking club was the Gargoyle in Dean Street, which was then owned by the Hon. David Tennant. Tennant was married to the actress Hermione Baddeley, and between them they knew 'everybody who was anybody' in London. For many years the Gargoyle was the late-night meeting place of café society and stage, political and literary names. For Burgess, the atmosphere of the Gargoyle was the very stuff of life itself, and he was a familiar figure there during and immediately after the war. The club has, incidentally, long since changed hands. Had he been able to improve his untidy private life there is some evidence that with the powerful support of people like McNeil and Jebb, Burgess might have made the grade as a diplomat. Indeed, after his stint as one of McNeil's aides, he was bringing pressure to bear to get himself transferred from the Junior Branch 'B' to the higher rating of Branch 'A'.

The Foreign Office would not agree to this, on the grounds of his extremely limited experience. He countered by asking to be moved to a political department, specifying that, if possible, he would like the Far Eastern Department, which dealt with China – a country in which he was deeply interested and on which he claimed to be something of an expert. It was also, incidentally, one of the few areas in which he found himself in agreement with British policy. Recognition of Communist China was, with his background, obviously a policy with which he could find little to quarrel. The failure of the Americans to do so was one of the principal reasons for his bitter and openly-voiced antagonism to them.

Of the few months he worked on Far Eastern affairs Burgess said:

'Anybody could be proud of the wisdom, the knowledge and the lack of prejudice of that department and the people in it.' He also found it extremely agreeable that his colleagues, with one exception, were all Old Etonians. His own behaviour, however, brought his appointment to an early close.

In the autumn of 1949 he took his leave abroad, touring in North Africa. With his insatiable appetite for involving himself in affairs which were not his concern, he made a point of calling on the various Secret Service representatives in places which he visited. And not only calling. He took the opportunity of impressing them with his own inside knowledge, making it at the same time unmistakably clear that his opinion of the British Secret Service in general, and the representative to whom he was talking at the time in particular, was not of the highest.

Not unnaturally, when he returned to duty in the Far Eastern Department it was to find that he was on the carpet. The various people he had visited had wasted no time in reporting what he had said.

So serious were the charges that a disciplinary Board was set up to investigate the matter. The charge was that he had been guilty of 'serious indiscretion about intelligence matters'. He was severely reprimanded. At the same time he was told that his services would no longer be required in the Far Eastern Department, and that his prospects of promotion had been diminished.

Nevertheless Hector McNeil continued to take upon himself the task of forwarding his protégé's career. He considered that it was of vital importance for Burgess to serve in an Embassy abroad. Burgess agreed in principle, but his enthusiasm was tempered by the thought of leaving London, which he used to claim was the only capital in the world where life was supportable. He could think of no Embassy where the life would appeal to him.

In due course, the posting came through. In view of all that was, or ought to have been known of Burgess, the selection of the first Embassy where he was to serve is practically unbelievable. It was Washington. In the Fifties the Americans did not take kindly to homosexuals.

Donald and Melinda's life in London during the worst of the Blitz had put their marriage under severe strain. Melinda, in particular, found the combination of German bombs and Donald's drinking bouts almost intolerable. When, in April 1944, Donald was appointed to the Washington Embassy, hope, for Melinda at least, flared again. For Donald the job as First Secretary was promotion. For her it meant a return to her homeland, her mother, her sisters and the possibility of a saner, less worrying way of life.

Donald's attitude towards her when they first reached America was strange. She was pregnant and he left her with her mother while he went to Washington. He shared an apartment with a colleague and claimed that he could not find suitable accommodation for his wife to join him. Yet the Embassy would have found them a place to live if he had asked them to do so; even if prices were high he could have had his housing allowance stepped up. He rarely sent her money, forcing her to live off her wealthy mother, although he knew she disliked being put in that position.

In the autumn of 1944 their first child, Donald Fergus, was born by a Caesarian operation and Maclean's attitude changed. He was thrilled with the baby. He went back to Washington, found an apartment, and brought his wife and baby son to live with him. They were together for Christmas.

Though his personal life was unsettled, his professional career was gratifyingly stable. The promise of his earlier years was becoming reality, and he was promoted again, to acting Counsellor and Head of Chancery. He seemed certain, at the war's end, to enjoy a long and distinguished life in the Foreign Service.

His new position in the Embassy was an important one. He saw most of the documents received and dispatched, and at this time they included a vast amount of correspondence and memoranda of the highest scientific and political importance. British and American scientists had worked in close cooperation on the atomic bomb that blasted Japan out of the war, and in the following years the secrets of that bomb were the subject of delicate diplomatic negotiation between Britain and America. Soviet agents were making desperate efforts to discover not only the scientific processes for making the bomb but the political policies of the Western atomic powers.

Maclean was in a unique position to help them, as, many years later, MI5 came to suspect that he had done. His private life about this time underwent yet another change, and if, as some of his friends believe today, this was the period when he first worked actively for Russia, this change may have had considerable bearing on it. Certainly, he became violently anti-American and began to drink more heavily than ever.

It was a time when Britain and America had done a smart about-turn on Russia. From the wartime 'gallant Soviet allies' they had become the peacetime 'menace to the civilized world'. And Maclean was now in a country that regarded communism as a dirty word. For a man who had studied Russia so closely in the early Thirties and who had obviously been so much in sympathy with communism, Western policy was certain to produce a bitter reaction in his mind.

Maclean's heavy drinking, his occasional homosexual tendencies and his sour outlook on America made him vulnerable to a skilled Soviet agent. It is quite likely that he had never lost touch with the Party anyway, but his disagreement with American policy could have done much, at this time, to inflame him to an active rather than a passive role.

What had he to offer as a Soviet agent? A great deal, although after his disappearance the Foreign Office was at pains to undervalue his knowledge. Indeed, there were denials that he was in possession of atomic secrets. This was true – if by atomic secrets was meant the hard scientific and technical information that Nunn May, Fuchs and Pontecorvo had already given to the Russians. Maclean's knowledge was of the political background. This was every bit as important, for by this time the Russians were already far advanced in the scientific field.

He knew the general heads of agreement between Great Britain, Canada and the US; he knew the points of divergence; he knew the reasons for cooperation in some fields and the lack of it in others. He knew how many atomic bombs we had, the amounts of uranium 235 available and the manufacturing potential with existing resources and materials.

'My God,' exclaimed Dean Acheson when first told the news of Maclean's defection, 'he knew everything!'

This statement was hastily modified, but the reaction was significant. It also contrasts strangely with the statement made by Herbert Morrison in the House of Commons shortly after the disappearance. Asked specifically whether Maclean had in his possession any atomic secrets, he categorically denied that he had. What he meant was that by the time he defected his knowledge of allied atomic policy was more than three years out of date. But Dean Acheson's statement was correct. During his years in the Washington Embassy Maclean had known everything the Russians most wanted to discover.

One of the positions of extreme responsibility which Maclean held as part of his Embassy duties was Secretary to the Combined Committee on Atomic Development. With this job went a pass which admitted him to the Atomic Energy Commission offices at any time of the day or night. He devoted himself studiously to the study of the political aspects of atomic energy, and was regarded by the Foreign Office as their expert on this subject. It was one which many of his colleagues found highly technical and deeply dull. They were glad he was prepared to take it on.

For Melinda, the four years in America were miserable. Maclean neglected her, vented his anger against America on her, and she had to continue to suffer from his excessive drinking. But, as in the Blitz on Britain, she bore her troubles bravely.

Their second child was born in July 1946. She went to New York again for the birth and again it was a son, Donald Marling. The child was two in 1948 when Maclean was appointed Head of Chancery in Cairo and the family sailed to England in September for home leave before Maclean took up his new post. Both Donald and Melinda were delighted at first when he was transferred. He was happy to leave the America he loathed, and Melinda was eagerly looking forward to a new life. With characteristic resilience the disappointment of her American hopes was already forgotten. But the cracks in the Maclean façade, first visible in America, were now beyond repair; in Cairo the façade crumbled completely.

Their home in the Egyptian capital was three-storied, big and spacious, the garden filled with luxurious flowers and plants, tall trees providing welcome shade from the sun. It was a house built for senior British officials, furnished and maintained by the government. The Macleans had four servants, gardeners and an English governess for the children. Cairo could have been idyllic for them.

Melinda was happy enough at the outset. Donald seemed to have settled down in his new post and to be enjoying his work. She quickly made many friends on the eternal cocktail party round and she was asked at short notice to arrange a party for the Duke of Edinburgh. He was visiting Cairo, staying at the British Embassy, and the party was planned to relieve the monotony of the stiff and starchy official programme. It was held at the Maclean home in Gezira and the guests were drawn from Cairo's younger element. Fourteen sat down to dinner with the Duke; other guests came in after the meal. It was a party at which they played such games as 'Murder', and it proved riotously successful. It was a social triumph for the once-shy girl from Chicago.

But after about six months, Maclean began to dislike Egypt. He contrasted the affluence and the social whirl of the few with the miserable poverty of the many. He despised the arrogance and ostentation so often to be seen. His communist soul revolted. He objected, too, to British policy in the Canal Zone; he considered the wait-and-see attitude stupid; he thought Britain should urge the Egyptian government to reform the social structure of the country and attempt to ease the misery of the masses.

So he began to drink again. Only this time his drinking bouts were much more serious than they had been in Washington. They led to troubles in the home and incidents outside which could not be hushed up. People began to talk.

One of the first incidents found him in a drunken stupor on a park bench without his shoes. That could be laughed off as an isolated incident, the result of a gruelling stint at the Embassy, and for several months all was well.

The next outbreak was far more serious. It happened when Melinda's sister Harriet came to stay with them. One day Melinda gathered a party of eight and hired a felucca to sail the fifteen miles to Helwan to visit friends who had a house on the banks of the Nile. There was plenty to drink on the wide-sailed boat, though little to eat, for they expected to have dinner when they arrived. But the wind dropped and the boat was almost becalmed; the trip took eight hours instead of the two that would have been the normal journey time. Maclean found consolation in the bottles on board. When they arrived, he was paralytically drunk.

Before the party reached Helwan, they had an example of what to expect from him. He picked a quarrel with Melinda, seized her round the neck and began to squeeze. The rest of the party dragged him away from her: she might have been strangled if they had not been close at hand.

It was about 2 am when the boat drew into the bank at their destination, and the party was far from quiet. An alarmed river guard challenged them as they stepped ashore and the drunken Maclean immediately attacked him. He pulled the guard's loaded rifle from his hands, threatening to smash his skull. A Foreign Office colleague, Lees Mayall, tried to stop Maclean and to get the gun from him. Maclean refused to hand it over, and the two began struggling on the river bank, then slipped and both fell on to a wooden jetty. Maclean landed on top, and Mayall had a leg broken in the fall.

The friends they had gone to visit would not let them into the house after hearing Maclean's drunken shouting and presumably did not believe the story of Mayall's plight. Eventually they managed to hire a car to take them back to Cairo. They arrived there just before Maclean and Mayall were due to report for duty at the Embassy in the morning.

A few months afterwards, Maclean invited a journalist friend, Philip Toynbee, to stay with them and the presence of an old drinking companion led to the worst episode of Maclean's Cairo days. Melinda's sister Harriet was still staying with the Macleans and Toynbee made up a foursome. One evening they all set off to a cocktail party. Melinda, who was not well, left early, and Toynbee went to an engagement of his own, leaving Maclean and Harriet to go to another party.

By midnight, Maclean was drunk and Harriet, bored with it all, decided to leave. Maclean stayed on drinking. About 2 am, he returned home, picked up Toynbee, and together they went out on the town. Many more drinks and a few nightclubs later, with dawn just breaking, they thought it would be a good idea to call on an Embassy friend. He let them into his flat, saw their condition, gave them a bottle of whisky in response to their demands for drink, and went back to bed. Later, when he left for the Embassy, they were still there, very drunk.

During the day, when the effects of the liquor began to wear off, Maclean remembered that a girl employed as a librarian in the American Embassy had a flat in the same building. He set out to raid it and get more to drink.

A cleaner was in the flat when he arrived. He pushed past him and helped himself to all the drink he could find. Then he decided to tear the flat apart. He smashed a table, broke the bath by dropping a heavy slab of marble into it, chopped up some of the furniture and pushed as much of the girl's clothing as he could find down the lavatory. Satisfied, he rejoined Toynbee in the other flat in the building and went to sleep.

Melinda found them there that night. She and Harriet dragged the pair of them out to a car and drove them home. That was the end for Melinda. She decided that Maclean could not go on with his dangerous drunken orgies and that drastic action had to be taken to bring him to his senses. Next morning, she had a long talk with her husband and then went to see the Ambassador.

She explained that Maclean was ill, suffering from a nervous breakdown, and that it was vital for him to return to London for treatment by his own doctor. By now, Maclean's personal standing at the Embassy was suffering from the tales being spread about his drinking bouts, and the Ambassador readily agreed to Melinda's suggestion.

No time was wasted. Two days after the flat-smashing episode Melinda drove him out to Farouk Field and saw him off on a London-bound plane. That was Friday, 11 May 1950, and his spell in Cairo had lasted a mere eighteen months.

The following day, from his mother's Kensington home, he wrote to Melinda:

> I am so grateful to you, my sweet, for taking all you have had to put up with without hating me. I am still rather lost, but cling to the idea that you do want me to be cured and come

back. I am weary of making promises of being a better husband since past ones have all been broken; but perhaps if some technician will strengthen my gasket and enlarge my heart I could make a promise which would stick. Anyhow, you have been very sweet to me and I will try to give you something in return. I was overwhelmed with sadness at leaving the boys; I suppose it affects one particularly because they expect one to be there and have no means of understanding why one goes away; it is, however, I suppose bathetic rather than pathetic so long as they are happy; I know you will keep them so. I hate having left you with all the responsibility for the house, family, car, servants, and long to hear that you are managing all right.

He ended:

I think very much of you, my darling, miss you badly and love you. Don't feel sad about me as I will come back a better person and we can be happy together again I am sure.

The Foreign Office sent Maclean to their consultant psychiatrist, who recommended that he should go to a clinic for an unspecified period. But Maclean refused, explaining in a letter to his wife: 'I do not feel that I can face going into a clinic. Fear plays a leading part in my resistance but I also much doubt that there is any point in it.' Instead, he went to a woman psychiatrist who had been recommended to him. Oddly enough, the Foreign Office agreed and gave him six months' sick leave.

His drinking went on – some of his friends said they rarely saw him sober during his sick leave – but he went regularly to his own psychiatrist. Their talks were concerned with his drinking, and the psychiatrist is said to have told him that this was caused by a guilt complex, the result of his treatment of Melinda. He claimed he could not bear the sight of her; that this was why he drank; that it turned him to homosexuality. But compare this with his letter to her on his arrival in London from Cairo . . . 'I think very much of you, my darling, miss you badly and love you . . .'

Meanwhile, Melinda in Cairo was left in a state of worried suspense. She had to cope with a pile of bills Maclean had left behind, a large house to run, the rumours surrounding Maclean's sudden flight to London, and the doubts concerning his future. Her position was made worse when an Egyptian paper heard of Maclean's final drunken exploit in Cairo and published an account of it with a few trimmings added for good measure. It was good ammunition for the anti-British campaign and other Egyptian papers published the story. Whatever their private thoughts, her friends remained loyal to her and the Embassy officials were reassuring.

In times of trouble, too, Melinda could always rely on her mother. Three weeks after Maclean left her in Cairo, Mrs Dunbar arrived and took charge. She paid the bills, dealt with the servants, who had become idle and a little cheeky, decided that they should leave Egypt and spend the summer in Spain, and supervised the packing for the journey. That all took three weeks and then Melinda and her mother sailed away to Spain with the two children.

Maclean could easily have joined them in Spain but he made no such suggestion. He stayed on in London and kept in touch by rather irregular letters. After they had been apart for about four months, though, Melinda received a letter written when he was in a state of acute melancholia. He said he could not see why she should ever return to him, he doubted if he would ever be a good husband or a good father, and that Melinda and the children would be better off without him after the way he had behaved. Melinda immediately cut short the Spanish holiday, travelled as far as Paris with her mother and the children, and went on alone to London and her husband.

She found the melancholy mood was persisting. They discussed the outlook for their future life together and Maclean expressed doubts about their ability to be happy. She talked, too, with the psychiatrist who was treating him and with some of his relatives and friends. She realized how much they had both changed: she had become more of an extrovert and enjoyed mixing with bright, simple people; Maclean would have none of this and preferred deep, intense people and topics. But she was swayed by those who told her how much he was dependent on her; that he would be a lost soul in a wilderness of alcoholic unreality without her steadying hand.

Finally, they decided to try again. Melinda collected the children from Paris and wrote to her sister, Harriet:

> Donald is still pretty confused and vague about himself and his desires, but I think when he gets settled he will find a new security and peace. I hope so. He hasn't had any drinking bouts since I have been back, but I can see that the root of the trouble is still not cleared away.

Maclean told his superiors at the Foreign Office that he had no wish to go abroad again for some time and would like to stay in London. This was agreed, and he was appointed head of the American Department. In this position, the diplomatic social round made few demands on him and the temptation to drink was therefore reduced to a minimum. He arranged to start work again on 1 November 1950.

Their plan was to live well away from London. Maclean would travel to and from the office by train each day and the journey would discourage him from drinking in London when his working day was over. They began looking for a house in Kent and made their base at an hotel in Sevenoaks. It took them about two months to find what they wanted – a big, isolated house called Beaconshaw in the village of Tatsfield, not far from Biggin Hill.

Cooking, cleaning and the routine jobs in a house were new to Melinda – she had been accustomed to servants all her life and at Beaconshaw she had only one part-time help. She also had to tackle the vast amount of work involved in setting up a new home – the curtain-making, the carpet-fitting and the decorating. Outside, a large, badly neglected garden cried out for attention. The two children were frequently in ill-health, and to add to everything else she found she was pregnant again. She had little time to ponder on her marital problems.

Maclean began in fine style. On most nights he caught the early train to Oxted and drove the four miles from the station to Tatsfield, arriving in time for the evening meal. Melinda was delighted, and was looking forward to a new era of domestic tranquillity and stability. But as winter gave way to spring, Maclean gave way to temptation. Occasionally, at first, he missed the early train. The 'misses' became more frequent. Then he began to miss all the trains and to stay in London for the night. Once he was mixed up in a scene at a London nightclub to which the police were called. On several occasions Melinda heard nothing from him for two or three days.

By May, his drinking had reached Cairo proportions. Frequently, he arrived at the Foreign Office, reached into a desk drawer for a bottle of whisky and took a large drink before he could begin his work. And it was nothing strange for him to arrive at cocktail parties completely drunk.

His anti-American diatribes were as fervent as ever. One night, after a dinner-party in Chelsea where I was present, he asked a friend: 'What would you say if I told you I was working for Uncle Joe?'

The friend replied that he might regard it as a joke, or he might not. He would not know what to think.

'Well, anyway,' said Maclean, 'I am.'

There was an embarrassed silence for a moment, the friend wondering how drunk Maclean was, Maclean staring fixedly at the carpet. The remark was not pursued, but Maclean soon launched into a bitter criticism of current American foreign policy which became almost hysterical. The friend was bored; he had heard it all before many times, and when Maclean got into this state he was unmanageable and unstoppable. The remark about 'working for Uncle Joe' was a new one but not, he then thought, to be taken seriously. He can hardly be blamed for taking no action, though MI5 did not take this view later.

Another incident of the same sort occurred in the early hours of the morning, in the Gargoyle Club. Goronwy Rees was sitting with a party in a corner two tables away from one occupied by Maclean, who was now very drunk, staring with fixed intensity in his direction. He took no notice, and indeed at first did not even remember who he was. He had not seen him for many years.

Suddenly Maclean got up from his table, lurched over to where he was sitting and said in a slurred but extremely belligerent voice: 'I know all about you, Mister Bloody Rees. You used to be one of us, but you ratted.' For a moment it looked as if he were going to pick a fight. Then suddenly his legs crumpled under him and he was brought abruptly to his knees. There he stayed, his hands gripping the edge of the table and his large white face peering over the top of it; from which undignified position he proceeded to direct a stream of incoherent abuse. After a few moments of this he managed to regain his feet and stumbled unsteadily back to his table.

Goronwy Rees had, of course, been politically extremely left-wing in his youth, but he had never been a member of the Communist Party. The only explanation he could put on Maclean's words was that Maclean had thought he had been and had 'ratted'.

After Kim Philby's fright over the Volkov incident, his career as a highly dangerous double agent continued to prosper. He remained with MI6 in London and continued to run the Soviet Section. By this time he was generally agreed to be the stuff of which future heads of MI6 are made – in other words, on his way to becoming a real life 'M'. It was decided, therefore, that he needed the experience of a field posting.

In January 1946 he took up an appointment officially as First Secretary in the British Embassy, in fact as head of the MI6 station in Turkey. If the country held unhappy memories for him after his visit in 1945, he showed no signs of it.

On his way to Istanbul he took some leave in order to visit his famous father, then an adviser to the Saudi Arabian court. His next task was to rent an agreeable villa on the Asiatic shore of the Bosphorus in which to install his wife, Aileen, and his children. From there he commuted to the Embassy by ferry-boat. He had a staff of five MI6 officers and the necessary secretaries and clerks. His task was supposedly to use Turkey as a base for spying on Russia and the Balkans and to collaborate with the Turkish Security Inspectorate.

The Turkish interlude seems to have been an enjoyable one for Philby. He was popular with his Embassy colleagues, he travelled a lot, particularly along the Russian border, and his work was less demanding than it had been in London. He remained there until September 1949. Then came further promotion.

After a short period of briefing in London, the Philby family arrived in Washington in October and soon found a comfortable house on Nebraska Avenue. Philby's cover was again as First Secretary in the British Embassy and once more he seems to have been popular with his diplomatic colleagues. His MI6 office in Washington was considerably larger than the one he had run in Istanbul and the tasks he had to perform for his British and Russian masters were considerably more demanding. In the first place he had to liaise with the CIA and the FBI and gradually transfer MI6's loyalties to the former without undue friction. While he was still struggling with this problem he found himself appointed to the planning committee of a joint Anglo-American operation in Albania, designed to overthrow the pro-Soviet regime. As a result of a security leak, the planned insurrection was a disaster and many of the insurgents condemned to death. To simultaneously plan and sabotage this ill-fated venture must have been a severe test of his energy and ingenuity. He had an additional worry. He had been told before he left London that there had been a serious leakage of atomic information between 1945 and 1947. His job was to assist the American authorities in narrowing the suspects to someone who had been in the British Embassy at the time. Philby knew, of course, that the spy was Donald Maclean.

One way and another, Philby was already showing signs of strain before Guy Burgess was posted to Washington in October 1950.

Anthony Blunt had left MI5 in 1945. His career as an art historian and as the Keeper of the Royal collections is well documented, can have been of no interest to his Soviet friends and need not, therefore, be examined.

7 The Plot Unfolds

In October 1950 Guy Burgess arrived in Washington. It is from this moment that a chain of events started which linked the Cambridge Conspirators and began the Numbers Game.

Philby was in Washington and already under suspicion by the CIA, if not yet by MI5, as the traitor in the Albanian affair. Maclean was in London, and one of several Foreign Office suspects for the betrayal of atomic secrets many years before. Burgess was being given a last chance to redeem his Foreign Office career. Only Blunt was prospering.

A week before Burgess arrived in Washington, Sir Robert Mackenzie, Regional Security Officer for north and central America, received an extraordinary report from London. While the precise contents have never been disclosed, they were of a nature to spread alarm and despondency in Sir Robert's office, where it was rightly considered that the security staff had enough to do without Whitehall adding to their burdens by sending out unreliable, unstable employees with a taste for drink and perhaps for other things as well. For the report was a summary of Burgess's background and career, and it said enough about his personal life to make them look to his arrival with deep foreboding. Kim Philby cheered them up a little by promising to try to keep an eye on him. . . . He would put him up in the basement of his house.

The forebodings of the Embassy staff were quickly justified. Within a matter of weeks Burgess was in trouble. The Security Officer, Squadron-Leader 'Tommy' Thompson, carpeted him for what was officially described on the report as 'carelessness with official papers'. Burgess had left his office unlocked and a pile of secret papers scattered on his desk in his usual untidy fashion. They were not, in fact, Top Secret, or anything like it, but were confidential enough to be embarrassing in the wrong hands.

Burgess's reaction to this reprimand was one of apathy. He wrote the required apology on the appropriate form as though he was explaining where he had lost his chequebook. His attitude was considered to be more serious than the misdemeanour, and Thompson mentioned it to Sir Robert. By this time, as it happened, Whitehall had received a protest about Burgess's appointment from the Embassy, and a copy of the report about his first black mark was sent to Whitehall to back it up. There was no constructive reply to either, though the only reply which the Embassy would have considered constructive was one which would have meant his immediate return to London.

As we know from his friends, Burgess was more than unhappy in America, and this was reflected in his work and his drinking. His friends were, as usual, extraordinary in their variety. He spent some time regularly with Sir Gladwyn Jebb (now Lord Gladwyn) in New York at the United Nations, and, in contrast, with a man in Washington who was a homosexual of the most unsavoury kind.

Out of all the turmoil, mental agony and unhappiness which his short stay in Washington represented to Guy Burgess there is only one memory which he treasured.

Shortly after his arrival Anthony Eden paid a visit to America. Eden was not then Foreign Secretary so the visit was an unofficial one. On the other hand the next election was looming on the horizon and it was quite likely that he would again be in office in the near future. Guy Burgess was the Embassy official deputed to look after Eden.

After he left he wrote a letter to Burgess in which he expressed his gratitude.

> *Government House,*
> *8th November, 1950*
> *Ottawa*
>
> My dear Burgess,
> Thank you so much for all your kindness. I was so well looked after that I am still in robust health, after quite a stormy flight

to New York and many engagements since! Truly I enjoyed every moment of my stay in Washington, and you will know how much you hepled to make this possible. Renewed greetings and gratitude.

Yours sincerely,
Anthony Eden

P.S. Incidentally that very friendly footman hadn't after all searched those evening trousers very well for I found in them those dollars and this key – so sorry!
A.E.

Though he seems to have managed to behave himself during Eden's visit, Burgess could not keep it up. Tom Driberg puts his bad behaviour in Washington down to his sensitivity and emotional complexity, brought about, largely, by his reaction to British foreign policy and its subservience to the State Department. There is no doubt that many diplomats felt the same way, but it is fortunate for the diplomatic service that they did not feel themselves to be above discipline and outside the compass of good manners. Driberg overlooks the character assessment of Burgess from friends from childhood: he was spoilt and wilful. These childish characteristics were carried through into adult life, aided by a personality usually described as 'dominating'. So it is reasonable to assume that it was not entirely his distaste for British policy that led him to his American excesses, but also the fact that he was meeting opposition, and people who actively disliked him – and Burgess had always liked to be liked.

His intellectual freedom was curtailed in America as it had never been in London. As a member of the Embassy staff he was subject to closer scrutiny than at home. No longer could he obtain an ironic thrill by expounding outrageous social doctrines at cocktail parties – and by that I do not mean communist doctrines, for Burgess had a political outlook of his own which did not fit any creed, and which he altered at will and with great eloquence. He still shocked people, of course, and took a great delight in doing so, but in Washington and New York his views were taken more seriously than in Mayfair,

Soho and Chelsea, where so many of his listeners knew him as an amiable eccentric.

In Washington, cocktail parties usually included members of the FBI or CIA, and they listened with misgivings to the man from the British Embassy. Whatever the rights and wrongs of their political views and attitudes, the Americans can be forgiven, as they listened to Burgess, for wondering: 'Are these people hypocrites or fools or enemies?'

Burgess's reaction to this unfriendliness and hostility found expression in long, bitter memoranda to London in which he said in effect that no one at the Embassy was any use except, perhaps, the Ambassador and, by implication, himself. British policies were wrong, he said, the execution of them was inept and the people who carried them out were hopeless. He was quite unsuited to his post, he admitted – but with the inference that he was unsuited because of his intellectual superiority, and that if he had committed any misdemeanours it was simply because the whole business was more than he could bear.

Despite Philby's efforts to control him, Burgess stepped up his already appalling record of alcoholic and homosexual excesses. He was careless about official papers again, and was again reprimanded; he had a rather ostentatious row with Joe Alsop, the famous American columnist; his drinking bouts became more dramatic and his friendships more bizarre; he was invited to lecture on Red China in the South and was stopped three times by traffic police on the way.

The traffic offences were made all the worse because he had picked up an American homosexual with a police record. The State Department felt that this was hardly the way for a diplomat to behave. Burgess, typically, was full of bravado, maintaining that he was driving at 100 mph when the police charge said he was only doing eighty; and again, that the Americans were only kicking up a fuss because the governor of Virginia, where it all happened, was notoriously anti-British.

The complaints book was now full. In April 1951 the Ambassador, Sir Oliver Franks, sent for him and told him he would have to go, that he was a disgrace to the Foreign Service. Burgess took this calmly, even cheerfully. He spent his last few weeks in the Embassy library, reading.

The Security Officer, Thompson, told us in 1962 that when he first met Burgess he wondered whether MI5 were playing some incredibly deep double game, so obviously unsuitable and unreliable was he. It did not take him long to realize that unhappily there was nothing clever in Burgess's appointment at all, and his own objective then became the short-term one of how to get rid of Burgess before he had the opportunity of doing irreparable harm.

To illustrate some of the difficulties Purdy and I had in presenting the whole picture in our book, the following paragraph appeared in the chapter describing Guy Burgess's stay in Washington:

> His 'misdemeanours', however, soon took a more sinister turn. One weekend while he was in Washington he stayed with a British diplomat. After lunch on Sunday he went for a stroll in the garden. His host was troubled. He had received a copy of a report from London which was the result of the MI5 enquiry into the leakage discovered in 1949. The stage it had now reached, the Report said, was a heartening one: from all the thousands of employees of the Foreign Office and its associate offices, four men had been listed as being principal suspects.
>
> One of them – the principal one – was Donald Maclean. Both the diplomat and Burgess knew Maclean, and the diplomat felt that some terrible mistake had been made. Knowing that Burgess had been friends with him at Cambridge he sought his opinion.

What we were not allowed to say in 1963 was that the 'diplomat' with whom Burgess walked in the garden was Kim Philby, and that he was not spending a weekend in his house but living there.

Philby had known since 1949 that Maclean was a major suspect. He had known since that time that his inclusion on the list was not some 'terrible mistake', but that he was, in fact, the guilty man.

Burgess arrived back in London in disgrace on 7 May 1951. It was the first time he and Maclean had been in the same country since

Burgess had joined the Foreign Service. Now Burgess was suspended and, as a result of the report he had earned in Washington, his dismissal was inevitable.

When he was in Washington, Guy had met Michael Berry, now Lord Hartwell, a friend from Eton days. Berry had suggested that, if he resigned from the Foreign Office, he might look for a job in Fleet Street. He seemed quite keen on the idea that Guy should come and work for him on the *Daily Telegraph*.

For Burgess it was a time to take stock and to decide where he was going.

For Maclean the position was equally fluid, and a trifle more dangerous than the one in which Burgess found himself. In April the two-year-long security investigations to locate the leak of information from inside the Washington Embassy had narrowed the possibilities down to four men. At the beginning of May it was obvious that the list would eventually dwindle to one name: Donald Maclean's.

One of a handful of people who knew of this investigation and of Maclean's involvement was Burgess. Philby had told him the story as they walked on the lawn in Washington. The first person Burgess meant to contact on his return to England was Maclean. He did not ring the Foreign Office direct, however; the telephone might be tapped he claimed and he was compromised enough already without sticking his head into such an obvious noose. Instead, he called Lady Maclean, Donald's mother, and asked her for her son's private address.

This caution indicates Burgess's love of drama. He had a perfectly good and innocent reason for calling on Maclean without having to resort to this roundabout method of communication. He had brought back with him from America a paper he had written on relations with China. He wanted to discuss it with someone before submitting it. What more natural a person to choose than his old friend who happened to be head of the American Section?

Eventually, he contacted Maclean at Tatsfield and they arranged to meet for lunch, not, as one might expect, at either Maclean's club, the Travellers', or Burgess's, the Reform. Instead they lunched at the RAC, quite most unlikely club for two diplomats to meet. This was, of course, why they chose it.

Over lunch they talked about the information Philby had given Burgess in Washington. It was confirmation of something Maclean already suspected. He told Burgess that he knew he was being followed: 'They even bumped into the back of my cab when I stopped suddenly yesterday. I got a good look at them,' he said.

Something would have to be done. Burgess, as always, was full of confidence. It was a situation in which he revelled. The cloaks were on and the daggers were out. He would see that matters were put right for his old friend and Communist Party protégé of those carefree Cambridge days. He would ask his friend Anthony Blunt for help.

The two had been on the terms of closest friendship since Trinity College days and knew each other's way of living as well as any two men could. They had shared a flat immediately after the war and spent much of their spare time together.

There was a regular Monday night at the Chelsea Palace in the King's Road. Burgess adored music hall and particularly the Chelsea Palace, now closed. Everything that Burgess liked, his friends were required to like too, and each week, when the show changed, it was the time-honoured custom for Burgess to go along with a party. The party was always the same: a woman friend of long standing and intimacy, a man friend from MI6 and Anthony Blunt. Just before leaving for Washington he gave a party in his flat. A guest who was present gave me this description in 1962:

> There was Hector McNeil, then Secretary for Scotland; Mr Kenneth Younger, McNeil's successor at the Foreign Office, Putlitz the spy; Professor Anthony Blunt; two young men who had obviously been picked up off the streets either that very evening or not long before; a couple of strange women, two men from MI5 and one from MI6, and Sir Harold Nicolson.
>
> The party got off to a brisk start with a large quantity of mixed drinks. One of the young men then hit a guest with a bottle, and later on his companion went back to Harold Nicolson's flat and after staying for an hour left with his host's wallet. A detailed description of the remainder of the party

would be the same as that of any Bohemian Bacchanalian shindig; the important fact is that the guest-list included three security men, one of whom, at least, was a homosexual. According to John Strachey, this man was an active supporter of the Comintern before the war, but renounced his association with the signing of the Nazi-Soviet pact in 1939.

Burgess can have had no difficulty in convincing Maclean of the extent of his intimacy with Sir Anthony Blunt. Despite the suspicion attached to him, Maclean was in a confident, relaxed mood, cheered by Burgess's reassurances. At one of his weekly lunches with Mark Culme-Seymour at the Salisbury public house, off Trafalgar Square, Maclean discussed at length the domestic problems that another child would bring. Melinda's confinement was barely a month off, and he was anxious, as might be expected. He was also talking of obtaining a transfer in the Foreign Office, and went into detail. 'It could all have been a carefully-thought-out plan to put me and the others off the scent,' says Culme-Seymour, 'but nothing will convince me of this.'

The lunch, incidentally, was the last the two men had together; when the time came for the next one, Maclean was on the run.

'The only point that stood out that day was that Donald did not drink as much as usual,' adds Culme-Seymour. 'He spoke of wanting to indulge in a "lost afternoon" around the pubs and clubs, but from his general demeanour I gathered that this was not a likely possibility. I was naturally rather pleased, for Donald when he was sober was a most charming and entertaining man.'

There is yet another witness to support Culme-Seymour's opinion that Maclean, far from planning the flight weeks ahead, made up his mind on the spur of the moment. The late Cyril Connolly, the well-known *Sunday Times* book critic, was a close friend of Maclean's and lunched with him the day before he left on 25 May 1951. After the Foreign Secretary, Herbert Morrison, had made a statement in the House of Commons about the flight, Cyril Connolly wrote to him:

I was very interested to read your remarks about Maclean and Burgess the other day, because I knew them both and actually lunched with Maclean the day before he disappeared. The point I wanted to mention to you was that on that day I am sure he had no intention of leaving in the way he did.

He spoke to me so normally as to his private affairs, his wife's confinement and his plans for the immediate future that I am convinced that he was not then intending to leave the country. This makes me feel that, subsequent to meeting me on May 24th, he received some warning that he was under suspicion, and immediately left the country with Burgess. It may be, therefore, that someone in the Foreign Office told him on May 25th that you had authorized him to be questioned. Of course, it was not until the Foreign Office knew that the security service knew as well.

This letter is of great interest, but the last sentence makes a false assumption. The number of Foreign Office staff who knew of the investigation was very small indeed. It was neither the Foreign Office nor the security service in London who gave Maclean his information, but Philby from his MI6 office in Washington.

It is safe to assume that Philby knew about Maclean's Cairo escapades, his nervous breakdown and that he was now drinking heavily again. Foreign Office officials on visits to Washington might be discreet about the head of American Department to the Ambassador or to the junior staff, but Philby was a contemporary and had known him at Cambridge. Moreover Burgess made a point of knowing all the gossip there was and was likely to have given Philby a highly coloured version of Maclean's reputation. The news must have been acutely alarming to Philby. Could a man in Maclean's physical and mental state possibly stand up to professional interrogation by MI5? And how much longer would it be possible to prevent the field of suspects for the 1947 leakage from narrowing to one?

Philby, in his autobiography, claims that he discussed the problem at length with his Soviet contacts and decided that, because Maclean was doing such useful work in the American Department, he should remain there until the last moment. They agreed, he claims, that Burgess should be entrusted with the task of arranging for his escape.

I do not believe a word of it. The main purpose of *My Silent War* is to show the KGB as omniscient, miraculously efficient, paternalistic employers who looked after their own and who had no difficulty in outwitting the bumbling old fogeys at MI5 and the FBI. Philby's story does not stand up to the most cursory examination. My own theory fits many more of the known facts. I believe that CIA suspicion and the leakage of information over the Albanian operation had so compromised Philby's position that the Russians had told him to lie low and break all contacts for the time being. Perhaps he had an alarm button he could press if he himself wanted to be spirited behind the Iron Curtain, but no regular channel of communication with Moscow or the Russian Embassies in Washington and London. If he had had he would not have used Burgess, his recent house guest, or the previously unsuspected Blunt, to get Maclean away. Apart from anything else, if Burgess was found out it was bound to throw suspicion on to Philby immediately. Burgess would never even have been told about the investigation into Maclean's earlier activities if there had been any alternative.

According to Philby, Burgess deliberately had himself sent home in disgrace in May 1951 on KGB instructions in order to arrange for the Russian Embassy in London to get Maclean away. But Burgess's bad behaviour had started many months before. There is also the curious fact that he lingered on in Washington and New York for several weeks after the Ambassador had told him he must go, then took a boat rather than an aeroplane. Had things been as carefully planned as Philby pretends, Burgess could have flounced out of the Washington Embassy and been back in London within forty-eight hours. Instead nearly two months elapsed between the Franks interview and the flight.

Nor is it possible to believe Philby's assertion that the KGB decided that Maclean must be left in place for as long as possible since he was doing such invaluable work. He had been of only very minor use to the Russians since his departure for Cairo in 1949. Andrew Boyle claims that the Russian agent, whose job it was to advise MacLean on what atomic information would be most useful to the Russians, had been 'turned' and become a double agent on the CIA payroll six months after Maclean became secretary to the atomic committee.

THE PLOT UNFOLDS

The newspaper's candidate for the role of the man Boyle called 'Basil' in his book does not seem to have overlapped with Maclean in Washington. This does not necessarily mean that there was not such a man. If there was, Maclean's reports, even from Washington, must have been of doubtful value.

Maclean's current job as head of the American Department sounded impressive but was virtually a sinecure, of no operational importance. He was given it to allow the Foreign Office a certain amount of breathing space before coming to a decision about his future. He was not on the circulation list of very secret documents and he was being followed very obviously. Probably MI5 were trying to panic him into defecting, contacting the Russians or confessing and agreeing to be turned. Yet Philby asks us to believe that the Russians in London knew none of this, that Maclean had no means of telling them, and that Burgess had to be used to inform Maclean of the immediacy of his danger. Does he expect us to believe that there was no means of communication between KGB agents in Washington and London which would have been quicker and more reliable?

The only conclusion to be drawn is that Philby was not, as he pretends, constantly and carefully cherished by his Russian friends either in 1951 or later in his career. The flight of Burgess and Maclean and the involvement of Blunt was a botched job, badly arranged by a man on his own and in a panic.

8 Day of Departure

Burgess and Maclean awoke on the morning of Friday, 25 May 1951, with no inkling of the dramatic events the day would bring. Maclean caught his usual morning train, walked from Charing Cross to his office, said good morning to the doorkeepers, hung up his hat and umbrella and settled down to work.

Burgess surfaced in more leisurely fashion. Since his suspension he had got into the habit of rising late, spending what was left of the morning pottering between his untidy, musty-smelling bedroom and the more comfortably furnished sitting-room. At 9.30 he was still in bed, the coverlet strewn with newspaper, stale cigarette-ends spilling out of an ashtray, a Jane Austen novel on the floor, a cup of tea made by his flatmate Jack Hewitt in his hand.

Hewitt went off to work, leaving Burgess attempting to find the address in Italy of W. H. Auden. He telephoned Stephen Spender, a mutual friend, but could not reach him; he telephoned other friends, but they did not know. He got up, bathed, shaved and dressed. At 10.30 he had an appointment with Bernard Miller, his current American boyfriend, to discuss a proposed trip to Paris that weekend. Now that he had given Maclean his warning and contacted Blunt he had not a care in the world; he had no ties, no job, and no responsibilities of any kind. There were three hundred pounds in notes in the wardrobe, and a young man waiting for him round the corner. Life looked good.

Just after ten o'clock, the telephone rang and changed his life irrevocably. It was a cable from Philby in Washington telling him in a prearranged code that Maclean would be questioned on Monday. The necessary papers were going to the Foreign Office that day...

There has always been a certain amount of mystery about exactly how Maclean knew that his interrogation was to take place on the Monday after his departure and about the fact that neither Burgess nor Maclean showed any signs of strain in the days that immediately preceded their departure. A plausible explanation is that Philby expected MI5 to take more time over trying to catch Maclean out and did not expect them to decide to pull him in for questioning for several weeks. The plan concocted with Blunt's assistance, therefore, probably involved Maclean asking for leave soon after the birth of his wife's new baby and taking off for Russia with all the family from somewhere like Switzerland. Philby was a professional, however, and would have arranged some innocent-seeming method of warning Burgess if things had to be speeded up. What they decided upon was a Western Union cable referring to Burgess's car, which he had left behind him in the Embassy car park in Washington.

It was Western Union's practice in those days to telephone messages through to the recipients, ask whether they wanted a confirmatory copy sent by messenger and, if the answer was no, to put the cable in the ordinary post.

Burgess would have taken the telephone call that morning, immediately realized that there was no time to be lost and, since he had to hurry out immediately to change Maclean's plans, told Western Union to put the copy in the post. It would have arrived the next morning while Burgess was on a boat . . . Blunt admits that he went to Burgess's flat to clear up a few things, but he must have called that evening before the written confirmation of the cable arrived since MI5 found it later and questioned Philby about it. Philby says in *My Silent War* that he sent a letter but his memory seems to have been at fault.

Burgess hurried to Piccadilly, hailed a taxi and drove to the Green Park Hotel to keep his appointment with Bernard Miller. They had coffee in the modestly luxurious lounge and walked through Green Park. Miller was excited and talked animatedly for ten or fifteen minutes about Paris and the friends they would meet there. Halfway across the park, with the grey bulk of Buckingham Palace looming up through the trees, Burgess stopped and faced him. 'Sorry,

Bernard,' he said, 'I haven't been listening, really. You see, a young friend at the Foreign Office is in serious trouble, and I have to help him out of it, somehow.' This, incidentally, was the first time that Burgess mentioned the matter to anyone, even indirectly. Miller was astonished, not to say disappointed, but Burgess assured him that if he could still make the boat that night, he would – but that he would not be able to say anything definite until much later that day.

They parted just before twelve, each rather subdued, for different reasons. Miller went back to his hotel, Burgess out into St James's Street on his way to the Reform Club.

At precisely that moment, Mr Herbert Morrison was receiving two callers in his huge office in Whitehall. They brought with them a dossier of papers which the Foreign Secretary read gravely. He put his signature to one, and the visitors left. They now had the power to bring in Donald Maclean for questioning.

As Burgess was entering the Reform, Maclean was on his way to Wheeler's to lunch with a young married couple. The place was crowded; they shared a dozen oysters and left. Maclean was in no hurry; his mind was apparently untroubled. They went on to Schmidt's, in Charlotte Street, for two more courses. He gratefully accepted an offer from his friends to stay with them while Melinda was having the baby, and promised to telephone the next week.

He took a taxi to the Travellers' Club, had two drinks in the bar and cashed a cheque for five pounds, as he often did at weekends. There was no one there he knew, and just after three he returned to his office.

In the Reform, Burgess picked his way through the lounge to a corner armchair, slumped into it and thought deeply. Many people remember him like that, with a large whisky that he was hardly noticing, at his elbow. Half an hour went by. He spoke to no one. Then, calling the porter, he asked him to get Welbeck 3991 on the telephone. This was the firm of Welbeck Motors, and from them he arranged to pick up a self-drive car. For how long did he want it? 'Oh, ten days,' he replied.

The switchboard then got him another number, but afterwards the operator could not remember what it was. This call worried the newspapers for weeks afterwards. Perhaps, they speculated, it held the key to the mystery. Who did he ring? Donald Maclean? His contact, whoever he was, at the Soviet Embassy? An agent or a helpful friend? Or the Fourth Man, later known to be Anthony Blunt?

It was none of these. He rang the Sunningdale number of Goronwy Rees, whose wife answered. At her end of the line his voice was thick and incoherent. She put this down to drink, but she was puzzled, too, for he told her: 'I'm going to do something which will shock you all, but don't worry about me. Don't worry.' He would have gone on talking, but she had no interest in a drunken monologue when lunch was in the oven. She cut him short and hung up.

At ten past two, Burgess arrived in Crawford Street to collect his car. It was a cream Austin A70, registration number VMF 196. He paid £25 in cash (£15 hire, £10 deposit) and drove back to his flat. He called in at Gieves in Old Bond Street, and bought a good quality fibre suitcase and a white macintosh. He saw Miller again, too, and told him that he would ring up or collect him at 8.30 that evening. At home, he carefully packed a tweed suit, several nylon shirts, shoes, socks, shaving kit and a dinner-jacket. He stuffed the three hundred pound notes and a bundle of savings certificates in his black official briefcase and carried them down to the car. As he went out, Hewitt came in from the office. Burgess seemed preoccupied, said goodbye, and walked out. It was to be the last time the two men met.

At 4.45 precisely, Maclean emerged from the Foreign Office and walked the short distance to Charing Cross Station, soon to be lost in the hurrying throng of men who looked just like him: black bowlers, black jackets, briefcases and umbrellas. Many were making for the same train, the 5.19 to Sevenoaks. Two of the crowd were not travelling; they were the MI5 men that he knew were there, watching. They turned as he passed through the barrier and went back to their office, as they had done so often. It was the same every evening. But this was to be the end of their particular trail . . .

Burgess arrived at Beaconshaw in his car barely half an hour after Maclean. The only help he could give his friend was to get him out of the country – and there were two boat tickets in his pocket. If Maclean had decided to go on his own, Burgess might well have driven back to London to keep his promise to Miller. Having given Maclean his boat tickets, he would not have been able to go to Paris, though he would still have had the car. It would have been easy for him to talk Miller into giving up the idea and going, say, to the Lake District instead – and, significantly, Burgess had actually asked for a map of the north of England in the Reform Club at lunchtime.

Whichever course Burgess took, Melinda would be questioned, and it would be dangerous if she said that Burgess had been there that night at the house. She had better say that she had never seen her husband's friend before, and that he had been introduced to her as Roger Stiles. While the police were looking for Roger Stiles, Maclean would be out of the country, and he would be either safely with him or innocently holidaying with his friend. It was a plan which appealed in every aspect to Burgess, with his schoolboy love of intrigue and the immense satisfaction which he got from a feeling that he was 'riding the whirlwind and directing the storm'.

Soon the three of them sat down to dinner. It was Maclean's thirty-eighth birthday, and it must have been an extraordinary meal. It started at seven and was over by eight. By nine o'clock the two men were out of the house.

The story which Melinda asked MI5 to believe later was, indeed, that she did not know Burgess at all, and that her husband had introduced him as Roger Stiles, a colleague from the office. She found him a most charming and entertaining companion at dinner, she said, and they chatted about all kinds of subjects, certainly nothing to do with communism, or Moscow.

When the meal was over her husband had gone out into the garden to stoke up the central heating boiler. On his return he glanced at his watch and said that he had to go out with Mr Stiles, but that they would not be gone long. No, she had no idea why they should have wanted to go out at that time of night, none at all. But she did not worry. She went to bed after tidying up the house (her relatives were arriving the next day) and slept. When did she expect her husband to return? Well, any time that night – although he had packed a few things, his razor and pyjamas, because, he had told her: 'We might have to spend the night somewhere.'

Melinda said that she did not really worry until her guests had arrived the next day, and Donald had not even telephoned to explain his absence. Still, she said, he was a strange man; he did strange things, sometimes. It was not until Monday that she made up her mind to telephone his office. In the afternoon, she spoke to Mr G. A. Carey-Foster, the Chief Security Officer (head of 'Q'), who told her not to worry – and not to talk about her husband's absence.

That was the outline of her story, and a very thin one it was; in retrospect even more so. After her initial call, however, her story mattered not at all to MI5.

After the initial shock which Melinda feigned, her life was in turmoil. Her first meeting with MI5 took place on the Wednesday following her husband's departure. It was in Lady Maclean's Piccadilly flat. Lady Maclean was in a state of shock, though being a strong-willed woman she managed to pull herself together to be as businesslike as possible in the circumstances. Mr Carey-Foster and two other men were there, as well as Melinda, who was treated with every sympathy and consideration, especially in view of her condition.

The meeting was brief. Melinda was given no hint of what progress the security department had made, if any, and she was approached as though she, too, was a victim of what had happened. She was, of course, though probably not an innocent one. Melinda answered questions in a very small voice, twisting and untwisting her gloves nervously, repeating constantly that she could not believe it. Again she was advised not to worry, and not to discuss the matter. She called on her doctor, was given sedatives, and returned home.

On that day her mother, Mrs Dunbar, came hurrying from France, aghast at the news that Melinda had given her by telephone the day before. There was nothing she could do, other than comfort her daughter, and hope . . .

Twelve days later on 7 June 1951, Melinda awoke to find that Donald's flight was a secret no longer. The *Daily Express* and, in the late edition, the *Daily Herald*, both carried front-page stories hinting at the scandal. There would obviously be no stopping them now. The next day, the two men were named in every newspaper in Britain. Her husband figured as the main news item on the early morning news bulletin, and by ten o'clock there was a long line of cars outside the house at Tatsfield. The local public house was besieged with reporters when it opened its doors, and continued to do a brisk trade for many days. Melinda all but barricaded herself in, refusing to answer questions or to meet the press in any way. That day she received a telegram. It read:

> Mrs Maclean Melinda. Beacon Shaw. Tatsfield near Westerham. Surrey England. Had to leave unexpectedly. Terribly sorry. Am quite well now. Don't worry darling I love you. Please don't stop loving me. Donald.

She phoned Lady Maclean immediately, to learn that she had received a similar message. She informed MI5 (who already knew) and gave a Special Branch man the telegram to study. Tracing it was a simple matter. Within an hour or two detectives learned that it had been handed in by a heavily-made-up woman at ten o'clock the previous night, to a post office in the Place de la Bourse, Paris.

One mystery which defies explanation even today is apparent in a *Daily Telegraph* report of 9 June: 'It was learned in Paris last night that the text released there of the telegram sent to Mr Maclean's wife is an abbreviated version. The full text contained eighty-two words. The French Authorities declined to explain why they omitted the missing words.' Heavy-handed censorship might have accounted for the strangeness of the wording.

Incidentally, Burgess's mother was not forgotten. A telegram to her, sent from Rome, read:

> Terribly sorry for my silence. Am embarking on long Mediterranean holiday. Do forgive. Guy.

At least the English was better . . .

To return to the evening of Friday 25th, the Austin carrying Burgess and Maclean sped down the winding country lanes from

Westerham, its headlights picking out the signposts that led to Southampton, a hundred miles on. They were late, and it looked likely that all their plans would collapse through missing the midnight boat to St Malo.

On the back seat were the suitcases, two of Burgess's (and his briefcase) and one of Maclean's. The conversation in the car can only be imagined – Maclean, no doubt, depressed at the thought of leaving his wife in a terrifying predicament, Burgess elated at the prospect of excitement. There was no going back now. It had all been finally settled in such a hurry that, perhaps for the first time in his life, he had deliberately missed an appointment (with Miller) and, uncharacteristically, not even telephoned to apologize. They arrived in Southampton at 11.45, fifteen minutes before the boat sailed. Burgess left the car at the dockside, unlocked.

On board the *Falaise*, they went straight to the cabin Burgess had booked for himself and Miller and did not appear in the bar at all. Next morning, they disembarked at 10.30 in the pouring rain on the grey quayside of St Malo. Burgess left behind, under his bed, the suitcase containing his dinner-jacket. He would not need that where he was going.

They had already decided to make for Rennes, but missed the train by minutes. At the station they caught a taxi and ordered Albert Gilbert, the incredulous driver, to Rennes, miles away. He drove as only French taxi-drivers can, and beat the train by twenty minutes. From there to Paris, from Paris, on the night express, to Berne. They sat in the station restaurant until the Czech Consulate Visa Section opened, and had their passports stamped for Prague, where an international trade fair had opened. By train to Zürich, then by plane to Prague, with two days' waiting in between.

This, anyway, is the now officially accepted story of their flight, and as far as it could be checked, it has been, with one snag. Burgess has claimed on several occasions that they stayed in an hotel in Berne, but he could not remember the name (and Swiss intelligence checked very soon afterwards), and not one possessed an alien's card in the name of Burgess or Maclean. And of all the countries in the world where (especially in those days) it was necessary for a foreigner to produce his passport at an hotel, Switzerland was the strictest.

Either they had false passports, or else they stayed at a 'safe' house or, perhaps, an embassy.

Two days before Maclean's third child was born, he and Burgess stepped off an airliner and on to Russian soil. The bridges behind them were burning fiercely . . .

With the advantage of hindsight this chapter, nearly unchanged since 1963, calls for the underlining of certain points.

Firstly it must be perfectly obvious that the haphazard circumstances surrounding the sudden flight were occasioned by the fact that Maclean had not intended to leave the country so soon. Second, it was obviously no part of anyone's plan that Burgess should go with him.

Blunt has now admitted that he did contact the Russians at this time. Whether he put them into direct touch with Burgess is not known. Obviously, however, whatever plans the Russians may have had for spiriting Maclean, and probably his family as well, out of the country, they cannot have involved Maclean very nearly missing a boat to France on which Burgess had bought tickets for himself and Bernard Miller. Sometime on Friday 25 May someone must have let the Russians know that Maclean's departure could no longer be delayed and that he was going to try to make his own way to Prague and that he would be stopping in Berne to collect his Czech visa. The explanation for the lack of a card in a Berne hotel is probably that the Russians picked up the two at the Czech Embassy there and put them up privately somewhere in Switzerland until their Prague plane left.

The next point that is quite obvious is that Melinda had been completely in the picture at least since the day of the escape (and probably long before) and approved of Donald's action. It is inconceivable, otherwise, that she should have waited until the afternoon of the following Monday before telephoning Carey-Foster, and even more inconceivable that Carey-Foster should have told her not to worry and to say nothing.

As it was intended to pull Maclean in for questioning on the Monday morning, when he did not turn up at the office, all the alarm bells should have started ringing frantically and the first action would have been for someone to ring his home to find out whether he was ill. Unless, of course, Carey-Foster knew where he was and was interested in seeing how long it would be before Melinda rang him. A security blackout was imposed which lasted for twelve days. When the story actually broke, everybody concerned could have been certain that Maclean was already safe in Moscow.

There is little doubt that Burgess had no real intention of joining Maclean in exile. It is much more likely that he thought that, having delivered the body to either Berne or Prague, he would be at liberty to return to London. It was probably the Russians who had other ideas. However reluctantly, they must have decided that as Burgess had gone so far he must go the whole way. Otherwise he would have become a security risk. He could and probably would have betrayed Blunt and Philby under skilful interrogation.

Blunt is now known to have played a part in assisting in Maclean's escape: someone with whom he had had little in common since the Cambridge days and for whom he had no personal affection. Burgess was a different matter. When Blunt learned that he had also vanished he was deeply upset for many weeks.

9 And Now, Melinda

It must have been with some relief that Melinda entered hospital on 13 June. Even the Caesarean operation she had to undergo, she joked later, was worth the few days' peace she had then. In the hours that she had to wait in the labour ward, Melinda wrote this letter:

My dearest Donald:
If you ever receive this letter, it will mean that I shan't be here to tell you how much I love you and how really proud of you I am. My only regret is that perhaps you don't know how I feel about you.

I feel I leave behind and have had a wonderful gift in your love and the existence of Fergie and Donald. I am so looking forward to the new baby. It seems strangely like the first time and I really think I shall enjoy this baby completely. I never forget, darling, that you love me and am living for the moment when we shall all be together again.

All my deepest love and wishes for a happy life for you and the children.

Melinda

Clearly this was written with deep sincerity and emotion, and with the stark fact facing her that the operation might cost her her life. One sentence is revealing, in the light of her protestations of ignorance: '. . . how really proud of you I am'. Whatever the assessment of her husband, it is impossible not to admire and respect Melinda, a woman of tremendous courage with deep convictions, who faced far greater dangers than Maclean, acting with the cunning and spirit of a lioness defending her young.

That letter was never posted. She eventually left it behind for her mother to find among her personal papers, twenty-seven months later.

On the morning of 13 June 1951 she gave birth to a healthy girl, and recovered completely and quickly. With the baby she seemed to renew her strength, and faced the inevitable reporters defiantly (though still telling them nothing). She said nothing, on direct instructions from the Foreign Office; she told friends that she would not have minded one Press conference if a bargain could have been made that she would be left in peace afterwards. This is an old bargain that has often been made by Fleet Street, and often (though not always) adhered to by newspapers.

The pressure on her from both the Press and the security men began to build up, as neither was getting anywhere with their separate inquiries. Mrs Dunbar, fearing that her daughter would have a nervous breakdown, found and rented a house at Beauvallon, near St Tropez, towards the end of July.

Another bombshell came just before the move, in the form of two drafts for £1000, sent on Maclean's behalf from Switzerland. They went to Mrs Dunbar; to Melinda went a letter from Donald. It was warm, affectionate and apologetic, and from the moment she received it, it was never out of her handbag.

Melinda and her three children set off for the South of France on 17 August with her mother, her sister Catherine and Catherine's child. They went against the advice of the Foreign Office and MI5, but Mrs Dunbar insisted, and as the journey was genuinely for health reasons the objections were withdrawn. For the first ten days, the villa was besieged by reporters and photographers, but they were gradually withdrawn until the whole family were left in peace for their last fortnight.

Melinda wrote to Harriet, back in England:

> Life goes on and gradually a pattern seems to emerge out of the swamp. Oh, I can't tell you how completely shipwrecked I feel. Like a drowning man, my past seems to rise up and confront me and I couldn't be more horrified. I made the fatal mistake of reading old letters (1939 ones, not Donald's) and as

far as I can see I never wrote and answered any of them and altogether behaved so bitchily or unconsciously that it isn't true. I can't tell you how shocked I am.

She ended:

... nor have I lost a particle of faith in Donald, but, oh, God, why is life quite so difficult?

With almost a year of separation gone, and still not officially knowing where her husband was, she spoke to friends of divorce, but 'discovered' that under English law she would have to wait three years before obtaining one on grounds of desertion. It seems unlikely that she did not know this already, but even to friends there could be no let-up in the pretence.

The move to Switzerland in 1952 made the coming Soviet intelligence operation much easier. Remembering what had happened the previous year, Melinda asked the Foreign Office for permission to issue a Press statement. It went to the Press Association, and said that she intended to live in France or Switzerland for the sake of greater privacy for the children. There were no assurances from the Press that she would be left alone, but one was volunteered by MI5, who also reported that they had no indications yet of where Burgess and Maclean were.

The beginning of September found the family in Geneva, with a small home in the rue des Alpes. The two boys started school, and life returned to normal, temporarily. Apart from one quick trip back to England to do some Christmas shopping and see old friends, Melinda lay low. On 1 January 1953, she wrote to Harriet again:

Thank God for the New Year. I couldn't be happier to see 1952 go. Mother and I celebrated quietly with a bottle of champagne and a miniature log fire and in our strange optimistic way we felt that perhaps 1953 might be better for us all. We survived Christmas once more. I am really getting to dread it and Mother and I could hardly wait to throw away all the Christmas decorations; only the tree remains. Next year I am going to send the boys away with their school friends on a skiing trip.

It could be that hope was fading for Melinda now; the hope that it would be possible to join Donald in Russia. Anyway, she discussed with her mother at great length the possibility of going to live in America. Mrs Dunbar was delighted at the prospect, and hurried off to New York with two principal objectives: to see if Melinda's American passport could be renewed, and to inquire about the possibilities of a divorce for her there. It was to be a wasted journey.

While her mother was away, Melinda was contacted by an agent of the KGB. Swiss intelligence believe this man was an American, who passed through Geneva very quickly, stopping only long enough to brief Melinda on the plans to get her out. On his instructions, she called at a photographer's shop in Geneva and had passport pictures made of herself and the children. She wanted them in a hurry, she said, and gave her name as Mrs Smith. The reason for the hurry was that her mother was already on her way back from New York, and actually arrived three days later, to be told nothing of this development.

The agent may have chosen the meeting-place, and if so, it is likely to have been the tiny skiing resort of Saanenmoser, near Gstaad, where she went with the children for two weeks. This is a probability only because she returned there later, for no good reason.

Mrs Dunbar was horrified at the change in her daughter on her return; she was strained, with a white face and the listlessness that she had shown in England. Her health, it appeared, had suffered a major setback. Gone was the excitement at the prospect of living in America again; she read only casually the papers and forms her mother had carefully collected in order to smooth away her problems.

The one incident which brought her alive again was the offer from a friend of a holiday villa in Majorca. Arrangements were made for them all to move there on 1 July. Unaccountably, two or three days before, Melinda changed her mind and cancelled everything, much to the dismay of Mrs Dunbar and the anguish of the children.

Instead, she announced calmly that she was taking the boys to Saanenmoser, instead of Majorca! There was no snow and nothing else to do there. What on earth did she want to go to Saanenmoser for? 'Mountain air,' Melinda replied.

On the day she should have arrived in Palma, Melinda and her baby daughter and two unhappy boys drove off on their improbable holiday. 'Back in a fortnight' were her last words to her mother. But she was back in five days. The weather had been bad; she had been completely mistaken, explained Melinda, adding that she would now like nothing better than to make the Majorca trip.

They did, and the five weeks they spent there in the sun made a tremendous difference to all of them.

The message was waiting for her when they returned to Geneva – on Monday, 7 September. According to the Swiss authorities Melinda went to the central post office and collected a Poste Restante letter. It informed her, presumably, that the operation to smuggle her out would take place in three days' time.

That afternoon, she wandered around as if in a daze. Mrs Dunbar, by now accustomed to her daughter's extraordinary moods, said nothing, but watched anxiously. Melinda went shopping for items that were unnecessary, and spent the evening writing letters to people she had not written to for months.

As they were going to bed that night, Melinda stood in the doorway between their rooms. Mrs Dunbar thought she looked ill and worried. Suddenly, she said: 'Oh, how I wish I had someone to advise me!' Her mother wondered if she were referring to the sale of the Tatsfield house, which they had been discussing earlier in the day. She told Melinda she had some experience with property and asked if she could help. Melinda just shook her head and shut the bedroom door.

Melinda appeared to be quite normal on Friday morning, 11 September. She had breakfast and went out shopping. From her bank she drew out 700 Swiss francs (£58), and paid the rent of the flat. She also paid a £5 repair bill on her car at the Fleury garage, telling the mechanic to fill the petrol tank. At 11 am she returned to the flat and told her mother that she had met a man called Robin Muir, a friend from Cairo, in the market. He had invited her and the children to spend a weekend with him and his wife at their villa in Territet. He had explained that she might have difficulty in finding the villa but would meet her in the lobby of a Montreux hotel at 4.30 that afternoon. The boys wore grey flannel suits and blue sports shirts, the baby was dressed in a new coat and shoes, Melinda wore a bright blue, three-quarter-length Schiaparelli coat, and at 3.30 pm they were ready to go. They would be back, said Melinda, on Sunday evening because the boys had to go to school on Monday morning at 8.15. Melinda asked if she should telephone her mother when they arrived at Territet. Mrs Dunbar told her it was unnecessary; they would only be away a couple of days.

Melinda was quite calm as she left with two suitcases and the children. There was nothing in her demeanour to indicate prior knowledge of the fantastic step she was taking. Mrs Dunbar waved them goodbye and said she would be waiting for them on Sunday and Melinda drove off with the three keys to the flat and the only key to the letter box.

Mrs Dunbar laid the table for tea at six o'clock on Sunday and then sat at the window looking out for their car. The hours went by. Mrs Dunbar became frantic with worry, particularly as Melinda had not even telephoned to explain their delay. But perhaps the roads were choked with traffic and they had decided to delay their return until Monday morning. She tried to console herself with this thought, but spent a very disturbed night.

With no news of them on the Monday, Mrs Dunbar went to the British Consulate and explained what had happened. The reaction there was only irritating: she was told that her report of their absence would go through ordinary channels. She tried to get the officials to appreciate the urgency of the situation. She failed.

Back to the flat went Mrs Dunbar and put through a call to the Chief Security Officer at the Foreign Office. The result was immediate. Two senior MI5 men were flown out to Geneva, the Swiss police were alerted, and the search began.

The following day, a telegram was delivered to Mrs Dunbar.

Handed in at Territet, and written in a foreign handwriting containing several errors, it said:

> Terribly sorry delay in contacting you – unforeseen circumstances have arisen am staying here longer please advise school boys returning about a weeks time – all extremely well – pink rose in marvellous form – love from all – Melinda.

Melinda's black Chevrolet car was found next morning forty miles from Geneva, in a Lausanne garage only a few hundred yards from the station. The police were told by the garage proprietor that the car had been left there by a woman with three children about 7 pm on the Friday that Melinda disappeared. A piece of paper stuck under the windscreen wiper said it would be collected in seven days.

The car was dirty, the speedometer broken, the cigarette lighter pulled out and left hanging down, and the battery was flat. Among the articles in the car were a cardboard box from a Geneva patisserie, the remains of a packed meal, road maps, and children's toys.

There was also a children's book on the front seat of the car. Its title: *Little Lost Lamb*. Inside the cover was stamped: 'Property of Norwalk Conn Schools, Washington School'. It was a book that Mrs Dunbar had never seen before.

The preface said:

> When the little black lamb scrambled up the mountainside by himself, he didn't think he would get lost. He was only having fun exploring. But when it was time to go home, there was no little lamb among all the other sheep. Then came a cry which the shepherd knew meant danger for all little lambs away from their mothers . . .

Perhaps this was meant to be Melinda's last message. She was certainly a little lost lamb and she certainly scrambled up a mountainside into the unknown when she left her mother in Geneva.

Melinda caught the 6.58 pm train from Lausanne to Zürich – a ticket collector at the station and a Swiss professor remembered seeing her and the children catch it. An American colonel shared a first-class compartment with them on the night train from Zürich to the Austrian town of Schwarzach St Veit, forty miles from Salzburg. A porter there remembered them leaving the train at 9 am on the Saturday. He said they went into a restaurant for coffee and about half an hour later they were driven away in a big American car. The driver was described as a slim man of medium height who spoke German with an Austrian accent.

There the trail ended. No one saw her after that.

For four days after Melinda's disappearance, Mrs Dunbar was too distraught to sleep. The initial shock was followed by realization of the significance of her daughter's disappearance: that she might never see Melinda and her grandchildren again; that the Iron Curtain had shut them out of her life for ever. She felt beaten and exhausted, and left for Paris to seek consolation from her daughter Harriet.

Five weeks later she returned to Geneva to close the flat in the rue des Alpes. Nothing seemed to have been touched in her absence, but when she began looking for Melinda's clothes she found nearly everything had gone. Coats, suits, dresses, blouses, sweaters, cardigans, skirts, shoes and underclothing – they were all missing. Only her mink coat and an expensive new evening dress were left in the wardrobe.

Someone could have been sent to the flat while Mrs Dunbar was away in Paris to pack Melinda's clothes and take them to her – she had the keys to the flat with her when she disappeared. But this would have meant gambling on the flat not being watched by the police and risking the possibility of being seen by the concierge. The more feasible explanation is that Melinda knew well in advance that she was joining Maclean in Russia, and packed everything she could.

Mrs Dunbar closed up the flat and went sadly back to her daughter in Paris. There, at the end of October, she received a short letter from Melinda. It had been posted in Cairo on 24 October and was written on cheap, greyish-blue notepaper.

It began 'Darling Mummy' – the usual way in which Melinda began letters to her mother – and went on to say that she and the children were safe and well and she hoped her mother would understand how deeply she felt the sorrow and worry her departure would cause her. They all missed Mrs Dunbar and would always think of her. She sent their love to her and to Catherine and Harriet.

'Please believe me, darling, in my heart I could not have done otherwise than I have done,' she wrote.

The letter ended: 'Goodbye – but not for ever. Melinda.'

10 Paperchase

The passages that follow are reprinted from our 1963 book.

The presses of Fleet Street devoured every word of the Burgess and Maclean story from the start, showing an appetite – and a lack of table manners – that shocked successive British governments, embarrassed the Foreign Office and thoroughly discomfited the Security Services. Why did the newspapers create such a fuss?

It was the time of the crumbling Image. There was a feeling in Britain, as distinctive as the atmosphere of the Thirties; a sick apprehension and uncertainty, a lack of direction and a suspicion and fear which added up to a national neurosis. The wildest weed of rumour flowered at speed, with only the lightest overnight watering of fact necessary. The very thought of two British diplomats fleeing to the Russians with an unknown quantity of secrets was enough to send shivers down Britannia's spine. Anxiety was heightened by the government policy of telling as little as possible, like a doctor with a deeply suspicious patient saying there is not much wrong.

The British Press determined to find out what was wrong, and mounted one of the largest operations ever undertaken by Fleet Street. Overall, it was the biggest newspaper campaign of the century up to that time.

It broke on the morning of 6 June 1951. Into the offices of the *Daily Express* went a curious, intriguing tip; two Foreign Office men had vanished, and were believed to be behind the Iron Curtain. The message was enough to alert *Express* correspondents in Paris, Rome, Vienna and Prague. By mid-afternoon, their inquiries had produced nothing. On the editorial conference schedule, the item remained, starkly, 'Foreign Office mystery'.

At 10 pm, Larry Solon, chief of the Paris bureau, spoke to the night editor. The paper's front page that morning carried four dramatic paragraphs that scooped the world. They said, simply:

> Scotland Yard officers and French detectives are hunting for two British government employees who are believed to have left London with the intention of getting to Moscow.
>
> According to a friend they planned the journey 'to serve their idealistic purposes'. One report says that the two men were employed by the Foreign Office and that there is a possibility that they may have important papers with them.
>
> News of their plan was given to the authorities by a friend, who said they expected him to go with them. They were to go to France as if on holiday, and make their way behind the Iron Curtain. The friend backed out.
>
> Several experts have flown from London to France to work with the French police. All French airports and frontiers are being watched. Plain-clothes men are searching the Montmartre area of Paris, where it is easy for anyone to hide. It is understood the police are watching visitors to the Soviet Embassy in Paris.

That was the start of the hunt. It is worth reading that first report again, remembering that the reporters who worked through the night met with nothing but bland denials or blank faces or furious accusations of scandal-mongering. 'Nonsense . . . completely untrue . . . rubbish . . .' were the official replies. Early the following morning came the first Foreign Office statement:

> Two members of the Foreign Service have been missing from their homes since May 25. One is Mr D. D. Maclean, the other Mr G. F. de M. Burgess. All possible inquiries are being made. It is known that they went to France a few days ago. Mr Maclean had a breakdown a year ago owing to overstrain, but was believed to have fully recovered. Owing to their being absent without leave, both have been suspended with effect from June 1.

The first incredible fact to emerge from the story – after the release of the names of the diplomats – was that Melinda Maclean was pregnant. It seemed fantastic that a Foreign Office diplomat, ex-public schoolboy and all that, should desert his wife so callously a few weeks or even days before the birth of their baby.

As each fragment of the tale unfolded, day by day, week by week, month by month, and – incredibly – year by year, it was obvious that much was being glossed over, if not actually suppressed, by the authorities. It began to look as though the powers-that-be were frightened of what might come out; so newspapermen pressed even harder for the truth.

All the resources of Fleet Street were thrown into the coverage of the story, and at one time or another most of the general reporters, political and defence correspondents worked on it. The *Express* offered £1000 reward for news of the two men. Its great rival, the *Daily Mail*, later raised the figure to £10,000. Executives of the *Express* estimated in 1962 that they had spent more than £100,000 over the years on the story, in everything from tips to the doormen of hotels to first-class air fares to Moscow.

The next story was that a 'large amount of money' had been sent to Mrs Maclean by the Swiss Bank Corporation and the Union Bank of Switzerland on the instructions of a Mr Robert Becker, who said he was staying at the Hotel Central in Zürich and gave a home address in New York. He looked, said a cashier later, like an ordinary American tourist-businessman. Swiss police called at the Hotel Central and drew a blank; no one of that name had stayed there. The cashiers were taken to the hotel and watched the guests going in and out without recognizing their quarry. The FBI in New York reported that the address of 'Mr Becker' was non-existent. Mrs Dunbar told MI5 she had never heard of anyone of that name. Nor had Lady Maclean or Melinda. Only the money was real.

The letter to Melinda from Donald that arrived at the same time was posted in Guildford, Surrey, a fact which helped not at all. For the newspapers the whole affair was a splendid mystery; for MI5 it was a sharp and unwelcome spur.

From the day that her husband vanished, Melinda was a figure of mystery; partly self-made mystery, understandably. She shut herself away in her home, refused to be interviewed or photographed, and made statements only through third parties – and then only to complain bitterly of the behaviour of Fleet Street men. With injured innocence, she proclaimed that she was being hounded unjustly; she knew nothing and could not help. The Security Services eventually appeared to believe her, and with gallant English deference to her pregnancy called off the half-hearted watch that had been kept on her house. In any event, whether she was believed or not, she had committed no crime. She had had no secret information to sell and, even if she had helped her husband to escape, there was nothing illegal in that. He had not been accused of any crime.

The Press were not so considerate. For months there was always a reporter somewhere in the vicinity of Tatsfield; all were convinced that one day she would lead them to news of her husband. 'Won't the bloody Press ever let this drop?' she asked in a letter to one of her relatives. The bloody Press would not.

From all the commotion over intrusion there came the decision of a dozen editors to leave the story alone, unless there were startling developments. Melinda Maclean was followed and photographed at the start of her holiday in France, to be sure (the late Geoffrey Hoare was very critical of this in his book *The Missing Macleans* published in 1955), but in the end there was not a reporter within miles when the couple established contact with each other again.

The British government stated in the White Paper: 'From information subsequently received from witnesses in Switzerland and Austria, it seems clear that the arrangements for Mrs Maclean's departure from Geneva had been carefully planned . . .'

The row over the 'intrusion' broke soon after the disclosure of the funds sent to Melinda from Moscow. It followed the Press Association statement on 15 July 1952:

> Mrs Melinda Maclean is shortly proceeding to France with her three children to spend a holiday of some weeks there.
> In accordance with the practice she has adopted since the

disappearance of her husband Mrs Maclean has notified the Foreign Office of her intentions.

She is hoping, it is learned, by changing her residence, to ensure a degree of privacy for her family of young children.

The men around the big news desk of the *Express* gave a concerted horse-laugh. One of their most experienced reporters was assigned to interview her immediately.

He did – on the telephone. But in the story which appeared next morning there were the dangerous words: 'Mrs Maclean smiled...' Something he patently could not have seen on the telephone.

It was a bad slip, but the repercussions were far more serious than he expected.

Every enemy of the newspapers – and of the *Express* in particular – flew into a righteous rage at this 'typical' example of newspaper villainy. Mrs Maclean fanned the flames by condemning the reporters and photographers (never identified) for badgering her children on the way home from school. Letters appeared in *The Times* expressing disgust at this shameful treatment of a poor woman who had obviously, and unwittingly, been the victim of circumstances. She was not responsible for her husband's defection; she knew nothing about it; she was whiter than white. Public sympathy grew and the flood of protesting letters that poured into the *Express* office left no doubt that many people felt strongly enough to cancel their subscriptions.

The row was still going on when Mrs Maclean slipped out of the country and made the secret contacts with Donald through agents in Switzerland...

The *Express* had learned of Burgess's attempts to discover Auden's address in Italy. The editor wondered why a man about to head for Moscow (if the rumours were true) should choose a time like that to inquire about friends in Italy. A reporter was sent to the sunshine island of Ischia to find out.

Auden did not know, and said so, but he had some revealing things to say about his old friend Burgess. 'Guy was a communist in the late 1930s,' he told the *Express*, 'and he was still pro-communist when he was at the British Embassy in Washington.' This was new to the public. He also disclosed that Alan Nunn May, the atom spy, had been a close friend and fellow undergraduate of both the missing diplomats.

Burgess, an inveterate letter-writer, failed to get in touch with his flatmate Hewitt, who quickly lost many of his friends, angering them by committing the unforgivable sin of talking to the newspapers. Actually they were being prudent, and he was not. To be publicly listed a sa friend of either missing man brought one to the notice of the Press and of the Security Services. For anyone to have visited Burgess or Maclean, however innocently, in the days or hours before their disappearance was to court searching inquiry, if not suspicion. No one wanted to talk.

The Russian Press was silent on the matter of the Soviet Union's latest acquisition. Every Russian diplomat who ever attended a cocktail party in the West was asked about the pair, but all feigned complete ignorance. In 1953 Mr Khrushchev himself, in answer to repeated questions from Western correspondents, denied point-blank that they were in the Soviet Union.

This was followed up, on 4 October 1953, by an article in the magazine *Novy Mir*, the communists' *New Statesman*. The whole affair of Burgess and Maclean, it said, was typical of the West's 'shameless methods of poisoning the international atmosphere. The campaign around the disappearance of Maclean is clearly inspired by the ruling circles of the Imperialist states', it went on, adding authoritatively:

> Insignificant in itself and having not the slightest relationship to the Soviet Union, the childish affair of the swindlers of the capitalist press, intelligence and diplomacy is an attempt to confuse international political events with the clear aim of arousing empty and even absurd suspicions among the most confident English, French and Swiss minds, and muddying the waters in order to fish out anti-Soviet fish.

Whatever the pros and cons of the endless arguments between journalists and officialdom, it was, nevertheless, the Press who prodded the government into activity, unearthed many of the clues, established and announced the whereabouts of the two men . . . and even found them in a Moscow hotel.

This particular incident is one of the most fascinating episodes in the background story of Burgess and Maclean. The reappearance of the missing pair, as abrupt and dramatic as their flight, took newspapermen and diplomats alike completely off balance – with the exception perhaps of one correspondent, Richard Hughes, the much-travelled correspondent of the *Sunday Times*.

Hughes had been in Moscow for ten weeks on a wide-ranging assignment covering the progress and prospects of the new Five Year Plan, and the meeting of the Supreme Soviet. And, like every other reporter, he also had the general briefing: 'See if you can find out anything, anything at all, about Those Two.' It did not take him long to discover that all the resident correspondents in Moscow were being constantly prodded by their home offices for the same thing. Nor did it take him long to become as frustrated, furious and frantic as they were.

Any inquiries to officialdom were either forgotten or lost – or met with the bland but definite assurance that nobody knew anything. This polite, brick-wall tactic, so much more efficient and infuriating than any Iron Curtain, was the end of every conversation with even the most carefully developed contacts.

There was nothing. Nothing at all. Blank. Nil. *Niet*.

Khrushchev and Bulganin were shortly due to make their famous B & K visit to England, and it was known they had high hopes of it. They wanted the best possible atmosphere to greet their arrival. It was essential that there be no rough patches that could not be smoothed over beforehand. They hoped for a great personal success and an increase in goodwill all round, especially after recent anti-colonial speeches by Mr K had been so sourly received.

To Richard Hughes, worrying at the problem in his room at Moscow's National Hotel, it seemed likely that B & K had been misinformed about the importance attached to the missing diplomats by the English Press. He reasoned that the Press-relations advisory group in the Kremlin had underestimated the interest in the mystery, and the annoyance which the constantly-made, rarely-believed denials had aroused. He felt that they did not realize that the first and last questions asked by British reporters, who are as persistent as any in the world, would be: 'Where are they?'

The importance of good relations, and all the diplomatic phrases, would be lost in this constant barrage, for which B & K would be totally unprepared. It could have led to lost tempers, harsh words – and the failure of their friendship mission.

He thought that if this point could be put to the Russian leaders simply enough, bluntly enough, rudely enough if necessary, it might make a tiny breach in the silent wall. The trouble was how to get the point in forcefully.

Suddenly and unexpectedly, Hughes was granted an interview with Mr Molotov, not then the sick, weary and discredited man he was later to become, but the powerful Foreign Minister. In the twenty-four hours before the interview he drafted and redrafted a memorandum 'for the eyes of President Bulganin and Mr Khrushchev'. It was not very long, but it was very much to the point. It stated firmly that the two heads of state must realize 'that the monstrous nonsense of this "I-do-not-know" formula would utterly discredit their pending visit to England.'

He said in his memorandum that an essential preamble to their visit was the appearance of Burgess and Maclean with some sort of explanation of just what they had done, and why. He pointed out that, failing this, it was likely that all protestations of friendship would be thought insincere, and that the stories would continue to circulate that the men were dead or in a Russian prison.

On Saturday, Hughes was waiting, not too hopefully. It had been a long shot and a lot of other methods had failed to have any effect at all. He started packing.

At 7 pm his phone rang and a voice asked him to go to room 101 on the same floor as his own, at 8 pm. Just on time he walked along the corridor to room 101 with the Reuters man, and correspondents from *Pravda* and the Tass agency.

They knocked and went in.

And there were Burgess and Maclean at last.

They gave no interviews but handed out prepared statements. Then, having proved that they were alive, in good health and spirits, they left. As Burgess handed a copy of the statement to Richard

Hughes he winked and said without any obvious necessity: 'We also want to give this to the *Sunday Times*.' There was only one front-page story the next day, all over the world.

The statement was short and anodyne. In it Burgess and Maclean described themselves as 'former members of the British Foreign Service' and gave their reasons for making it as a belief that speculation about their whereabouts was being used to undermine Anglo-Soviet understanding. They admitted that they had been communists since their Cambridge days but denied that they had ever, either of them, been spies. They had hoped, they claimed, that they could further Anglo-Soviet friendship by conventional means, using their influence inside the Establishment. By 1951 they had become convinced that British policy was so hopelessly subservient to American that there was nothing they could contribute to an East-West detente from Whitehall. By 1951 Maclean's open left-wing sympathies had led to the security authorities following him and tapping his telephones so he decided to go to the Soviet Union 'to further understanding between East and West from there'. When Burgess returned from Washington, as alarmed as he was about the growing and pernicious attitude of the American State Department, he had decided to accompany him. 'As a result of living in the U.S.S.R. we both of us are convinced that we were right in doing what we did.'

Tom Driberg, who had met Guy Burgess two or three times before the war when he had appeared on his 'The Week in Westminster' programmes, was an alert and enterprising journalist as well as a senior Labour politician. He at once wrote to Guy Burgess in Moscow saying he would like to interview him and write a book about him. To his surprise and delight Guy was enthusiastic, Weidenfeld and Nicolson commissioned the book and the *Daily Mail* contracted to serialize it. Tom Driberg arrived in Moscow in August 1956.

One thing Guy was insistent about, apparently, was that Tom should make sure that his text was submitted to Admiral Thomson, then in charge of the office which vetted the writings of officials to make sure they disclosed nothing likely to harm the government of the day and who issued the so-called D notices to the Press when a story was likely to be detrimental to the public interest. 'After all, Tom, I signed the Official Secrets Act when I joined the Foreign Service and I am still a loyal Englishman.' By chance Barley Alison, the person who handled the book at Weidenfeld and Nicolson, was a former Foreign Office official herself and readily agreed.

When she came to read the typescript it contained a fairly detailed account of the disastrous Anglo-American efforts to topple the Albanian regime. She pointed out to Driberg that this was certainly an Official Secret – and an Anglo-American one at that. He replied that Guy had been particularly insistent that he should include these paragraphs (and a passing reference to a secret department to which she had also drawn Tom's attention) since: 'Guy believes that it is a good idea to give the D notice boys something to take out – otherwise they don't feel they are earning their salaries.'

In due course, the charming Admiral Thomson made a polite request that these paragraphs be removed and they duly were – from the typescript and from every copy of the proofs. Twenty-three years later Barley Alison has only the vaguest memory of Guy's interpretation of the series of fiascos in Albania but *thinks* she recalls him naming one of the senior Albanian contacts as the double agent. With hind-sight it seems likely that Guy's motive for including the passages, for the eyes of the security authorities only, since he must have known that they would be removed before the general public read them, was loyalty to Kim Philby. He was offering an explanation of the fact that the communists had prior knowledge of every Anglo-American move which involved an Albanian and not an Englishman.

Perhaps Guy was trying to make amends for the fact that his flight had focused suspicion on his friend Kim: perhaps his Russian masters insisted on the inclusion of the 'disinformation'. Whatever the origins of the decision to tell Driberg about the Albanian operation may have been, it was a disastrous move for Burgess. Until that time it is doubtful whether MI5 could have made out a case against Burgess, the Russian spy, which would have convinced a jury. After 1956 the authorities had a tidy, water-tight case against him which might have earned him seven years in prison. He had disclosed Official Secrets to Tom Driberg.

11 Eleven Years After

If further evidence is required of official reluctance to disclose the full circumstances surrounding the departure of Burgess and Maclean and the determination of the Establishment that they should never be obliged to put them, Philby or Blunt, on public trial, I will quote some of the opening chapter of the book Purdy and I wrote in 1963. The scene we describe took place in 1962.

A black police car edged past the parked lorries of Covent Garden and swung into Bow Street police station yard. Two men stepped out briskly and, unnoticed by anyone, walked through a side door.

Inside, a large crowd of reporters waited. Some chatted to the duty sergeant; others sat on the oak benches scrutinizing the day's list of offenders, or stood staring out of the windows. There were more journalists than usual that day. Two wealthy company directors were appearing on a charge of living on immoral earnings, and the newspapers wanted every word of what was said. It was a slack period in Fleet Street, and news editors had to make the most of anything that was offered. If anyone had, therefore, wanted to find a large number of crime and court reporters that morning for any reason, then Bow Street would have been the first call.

In the spacious, book-lined office of Sir Robert Blundell, Chief Metropolitan magistrate, the two men from the police car were being handed by him a signed warrant for the arrest of Burgess and Maclean. The clerks and secretaries who quickly knew about the warrant were astonished. Had the missing diplomats come back, then, where were they? They knew that they would soon be reading the answers.

Det-Supt George Gordon Smith of the Special Branch, and Mr Peter Palmes of the office of the Director of Public Prosecutions, shook hands with Sir Robert and left, the warrant now in Smith's briefcase. But instead of leaving by the side door as they had arrived, the two men strolled into the main hall of the court building. Their appearance brought every reporter to life. The presence of these two, together, could only mean the beginning of something big.

'What's going on, George?' 'Anything for us?' 'Who are you picking up?' The questions came quickly as the journalists sensed that Smith was in a friendly mood. In one sentence, and with a twinkle in his eye, he told them what had happened. There were gasps and whistles of astonishment, then a dozen men dashed for the telephones outside: 'Warrants out for Burgess and Maclean. They are expected back from Moscow tonight or tomorrow.'

At 2.25 pm, Scotland Yard's Press Bureau issued this statement: 'There are grounds for supposing that Donald Maclean and Guy Burgess may be contemplating leaving – or may have left – the USSR for some other territory. In order that they may be arrested should they come within the jurisdiction of our courts, warrants have been applied for and issued for their arrest for offences under Section One of the Official Secrets Act, 1911.'

Section One of the Act deals with the gathering of information in prohibited places, the making of plans, sketches and models etc., or the communication of any secret official code word or password which is 'calculated to be, or might be, or is intended to be, directly or indirectly, useful to an enemy'. The maximum penalty is fourteen years.

Within five minutes of the Scotland Yard statement, teleprinters in Reuter's Moscow Bureau in the Sadova Samotochnyaya chattered out the news. Robert Elphick, head of the bureau, grabbed a telephone and dialled the number of Burgess's flat overlooking the famous Novodevichy Monastery. The call was answered by Burgess's friend, the curly-haired ex-miner, Tolya. He said that Burgess was away on holiday and would not be back for three weeks. Efforts to telephone Donald Maclean failed; he had changed his telephone number and taken on the name Frazer.

But John Miller, also of Reuter's, knew where Maclean lived. He drove to an eleven-storey block of apartments beside the Moskva river, took a lift to the sixth floor and rang the bell of the brown-painted door. A crew-cut youth with black hornrimmed spectacles, wearing a red shirt, answered. It was eighteen-year-old Fergus Maclean. Miller asked in Russian: 'Is Mr Frazer at home?'

Fergus answered in English: 'I will see.'

Maclean then came to the door. He snapped: 'I've got nothing, absolutely nothing, to say to you.'

Miller asked: 'Do you know about the warrant?'

Maclean looked over his shoulder to where his son and ten-year-old daughter Melinda were standing in the hall. Then he said: 'I've asked you not to come here. I have nothing to say. I've nothing against you personally, but I just don't want to speak about anything to anyone. Please go away. Goodbye.'

Two hours later Mr William Hatch, area manager in Amsterdam for British European Airways, telephoned his London headquarters from Schiphol with the news that Burgess and Maclean would be flying into London from Amsterdam on BEA flight 439, timed for touchdown at 10.10 pm. This message was passed on to reporters at 6 pm.

Fleet Street newsrooms immediately ordered teams of reporters out to Amsterdam, to catch flight 439 and fly back with the two fugitives. Blanket coverage was ordered for London Airport; high-powered cars and motor-cycles were lined up ready for the race into London after the arrest of Burgess and Maclean at the airport. Some went to Gatwick, in case there was a diversion of the flight. Extra men went to Scotland Yard.

Crowds of reporters, photographers, newsreel and TV men spilled out on to the Schiphol runway in Amsterdam when KLM flight 302 arrived from Moscow. That was the plane on which Burgess and Maclean were supposed to be travelling, before changing to the BEA flight. Arc lamps lit up the silver and blue airliner and armed Dutch police lined the aircraft steps. Out stepped sixteen passengers, bemused and bewildered by the lights and crowds. None of them looked like Burgess or Maclean.

One man was suspected and questioned repeatedly, but he maintained: 'I am John Edwards. Who is this man Burgess, anyway?' Eleven people were escorted to a coach and driven to BEA flight 439 bound for London.

In London, an impatient throng of Press, radio and television men were waiting for the 10.10 touchdown when the news reached them that neither Burgess nor Maclean were on the plane. No one believed it. Reporters continued to chain-smoke in the corridors and conference rooms; photographers checked and rechecked their equipment. Then came a rumour that the flight had been diverted to Herne airport. That was checked, and it was found that there had been a fifteen-minute delay at Amsterdam, but that the destination was still London. Still, some newspapers sent off more men to Herne, just in case . . .

At 10.30 the BEA plane landed and slowly taxied to its parking position in front of the long sightseers' galleries. In each oval window, clearly visible under the airport tarmac floodlights, was a pale face. The passengers could already see the batteries of cameras lined up at the edge of the apron and wondered who among them was the object of this extraordinary attention. As the turbines slowed to a whisper, airport police surrounded the aircraft, and two black cars drew up at the foot of the gangway. It looked as if the message from Amsterdam had been another bluff, that the diplomats were on the plane after all.

The television arc lights focused their hard bluish brilliance on the door as the steps were locked. It opened, framing a stewardess. Then came the passengers. One man stepped out, his head and shoulders covered with an overcoat. He hurried down, to be stopped at the bottom by the waiting police. The cameramen surged towards the group, taking pictures as fast as they could.

Was it Burgess or Maclean?

The man suddenly shrugged off his overcoat and laughed at the photographers. Then they too saw the joke. He was a *Daily Mirror* reporter who had caught the plane at Amsterdam and decided to pull the legs of both his colleagues and the police.

While all this was happening in Amsterdam and London, Reuter's John Miller drove again to Maclean's flat. This time, the door was opened by a middle-aged, bespectacled woman with a slight Cockney accent, believed to be the daughter of the late Harold Laski. Miller handed her a Reuter's message from London which said: 'A BEA spokesman said tonight in London that Burgess and Maclean are flying from Moscow on a plane scheduled to arrive at Amsterdam.'

Maclean appeared in the doorway as she was reading it. He looked very angry, and shouted: 'Shut the door! Shut the door!' The door was slammed in Miller's face.

So Maclean was known to be still in Moscow, anyway. But where was Burgess? His flatmate, Tolya, said after Easter that Burgess had telephoned him from Yalta and told him to tell callers that he had gone abroad and would not be back for at least three weeks. Then he began to worry about the effect of the mystery he was creating. He flew back to Moscow to clear up his position by issuing a short Press statement that he was still in Moscow and that he intended to stay there.

He phoned this to Reuter's from the twenty-seventh floor of the Ukraine hotel, from the room where Jeremy Wolfenden, the Old Etonian friend and correspondent of the *Daily Telegraph*, lived. That statement caused some of the fastest car driving that the Russian capital had seen for some time. Stephen Harper of the *Daily Express* tore across the city in his Ford Zodiac to see if Burgess was at his flat. Walter Lister of the *New York Herald Tribune*, who had been lunching with Harper, trailed him there. Tolya answered the door and said that Burgess was at the Ukraine hotel.

The two reporters then raced to the hotel and took the lift to the twenty-seventh. It stopped first at the twentieth, and John Mossman of the *Daily Mail* stepped in. He had gone direct to the hotel but had mistaken the floor number. All three newsmen burst into Wolfenden's room together – much to the consternation of their colleague and their quarry.

Burgess was lying on the bed, his Old Etonian tie loosened and his shoes off. He sat up, took a gulp of Canadian Club whisky and said: 'I'm not saying any more than I have said in the statement.' Wolfenden was putting typewritten sheets into the drawer of his desk. For half an hour, then, Burgess parried the questions expertly –

'I wasn't a Foreign Office spokesman for nothing, you know.' Finally they left him, to file their 'interview' . . .

In fact the reason for the sudden flap was that Dutch Intelligence had given MI5 a tip-off that Burgess and Maclean had been invited to attend a communist conference in Cuba and that, in the course of their journey, their aeroplane would land briefly at Prestwick in Scotland for refuelling.

MI5 quickly realized that this information was not in fact correct. On the other hand they had been disturbed for some time by reports that Burgess, in particular, was testing the water. He was asking what the reaction would be were he to return to England and, as he put it, 'face the music'. On one occasion I myself was asked through an intermediary what the reaction might be. I immediately informed St James's Street, then headquarters of MI5. I got a reaction of horrified dismay: 'For God's sake,' I was told, 'tell that bastard to stay where he is.'

It was because of repeated overtures from Burgess that MI5 decided to stage-manage the Bow Street incident with maximum publicity. After this Burgess could have been under no illusions about the official attitude.

The fact that the comedy was staged in London and not at Prestwick demonstrates that MI5 were ahead of the game and only anxious to make their reactions abundantly clear to Moscow.

In order to understand why, in 1963 Anthony Purdy and I devoted most of two chapters of *Burgess and Maclean* to Press reactions to the scandal it is necessary to remember that Lord Beaverbrook and his *Express* group of newspapers were a real power in the land at the time. They forced governments to make statements when they would rather have remained silent – and then they complained about them. Where they led the rest of Fleet Street followed. Lord Beaverbrook detested Anthony Eden. He had extended his loathing to the department Eden so often commanded. To be in the Foreign Service in those days was to believe that all the journalists Beaverbrook employed were paid to prove one effete, idle and dedicated to nineteenth-century concepts and practices. No wonder Foreign Office officials were defensive when two of their members defected.

Although no single newspaper in this country today wields the same political power as the *Daily Express* under Lord Beaverbrook, the incredible outburst of spy fever following the naming of Anthony Blunt, fuelled by the media and assiduously stoked by amateur spy spotters, has been an even less edifying spectacle.

12 The Third Man

The anxiety of our Secret Services to keep Burgess and Maclean out of England was not their only worry. They were equally concerned about who was left in. They would have been even more naive than they had been made out to be if they thought that, with the departure of Burgess and Maclean, the viper's nest had been cleansed. The circumstances surrounding their flight reactivated their interest in Kim Philby and Anthony Blunt.

Much the most interesting at that time, however, was Kim Philby. James Angleton of the CIA, whose suspicions about Philby were aroused at the time of the Albanian affair, had become even more suspicious as a result of a tipoff he had received from Jewish Intelligence. He was baying for blood. It was all immensely embarrassing in view of Philby's high position in MI6, and the loyalty of many of his friends, but action had to be taken.

Shortly after the departure of Burgess and Maclean, Philby was summoned back to London for interrogation. MI5 asked whether he would be a good boy and resign. Philby, certain that MI5 did not have anything really concrete against him, refused. There was also the consideration that some of his MI6 colleagues believed implicitly in his innocence.

Whilst Maclean's role between 1944 and 1949 should not be underestimated, his career as a Soviet spy or as a member of the Foreign Office was virtually at an end. To let him go without interrogation was acceptable. He had nothing up to date or valuable to give away. Philby's importance was greater. He could not be 'pushed out' without a determined attempt to break him, or the passage of a lot more time.

The authorities did not give up after the first interrogation but bided their time. In June 1952, Philby underwent what was virtually a 'secret trial'. First Sir Dick White had tried to achieve a breakthrough with his mixture of courtesy and toughness, then Helenus Milmo QC, a still tougher interrogator, and finally the most experienced interrogator of them all, William Skardon. Philby's resource and verbal agility defeated them all.

It was then that Dick Brooman-White, a newly elected MP, persuaded the then head of MI6 that the time had come to call off the hunt and plaster over the cracks. Although officially declared to be in the clear, it was obvious that Philby's usefulness to MI6 (or for that matter the Russians) had gone. Like the other two before him, he was neutralized, and there the matter might have rested but for the sudden admission in February 1956 that Burgess and Maclean were indeed in Moscow. Immediately the uproar started all over again.

The government were forced into the position of issuing a White Paper. It was published in September 1955 and was little more than a potted biography of the two men and a rather wishy-washy admission that after the defection of Vladimir Petrov, a former Third Secretary of the Soviet Embassy, on 3 April 1954, there was some reason for believing that Burgess and Maclean might have been agents for the KGB. Possibly the most fatuous part of the whole White Paper read:

> Petrov himself was not directly concerned in the case and his information was obtained from conversation with one of his colleagues in Soviet service in Australia. Petrov states that both Maclean and Burgess were recruited as spies for the Soviet Government while students at University, with the intention that they should carry out their espionage tasks in the Foreign Office, and that in 1951, by means unknown to him, one or other of the two men became aware that their activities were under investigation.

This pathetic attempt at a whitewash only increased the fury of the Press in particular and the high indignation of the public in general. To gauge the measure of its failure and the weight of public belief in conspiracy and collusion, it is helpful to read the opinion of *The Times*, which might have been expected to mend the broken fences of the Establishment. Instead, this appeared, under the heading of 'Too Little and Too Late':

> 'Two points call for comment' says the White Paper on Maclean and Burgess. That is typical of its primness and defensiveness. There are not two but a dozen points that call for comment, and the White Paper throws little new light on them.
>
> Appearing as it does, scandalously late, four and a quarter years after the two men fled the country, the White Paper might have been expected to give many details hitherto unknown.
>
> Throughout the past four and a quarter years the pattern has been invariably the same. A Press report has been followed by a reluctant and often tendentious admission in the House or at the Foreign Office.

The *Daily Telegraph* called the White Paper 'a total failure', the *Daily Mail*, 'alarming', the *News Chronicle*, 'laughable, were the whole thing not so serious'. The *New Statesman* declared that 'the White Paper reveals nothing but incompetence'. Richard Crossman in the *Daily Mirror* wrote: 'it makes it clear that many of the answers which Ministers were briefed to give were deliberate suppressions of the truth – and some were actual lies'. The *Daily Express* asked, simply: 'Who are the guilty men?'

The matter was not to be allowed to die down. On 25 October 1955, Lt Colonel Marcus Lipton MP had put a question to the Foreign Secretary (Mr Macmillan) in which he asked whether he would investigate the part played by Mr H. A. R. Philby in the defection of the two men now generally known as the Foreign Office spies. On 7 November Macmillan initiated a debate on the disappearance of Burgess and Maclean. When it came to Marcus Lipton's allegations about Philby, *The Times* summarized his reply:

> The name of one man has been mentioned in the House, but

not outside, in this connexion. He was Mr H. A. R. Philby, temporary First Secretary to the British Embassy in Washington from October, 1949 to June, 1951, who had been privy to much of the investigation of the leakage. He had been friends with Burgess from their time as fellow undergraduates in Trinity College, Cambridge, and Burgess was accommodated at his home in Washington from August, 1950 to April, 1951. It would be realised that at no time before he fled was Burgess under suspicion. It had been found that Mr Philby had Communist associations before and after his university days, and he was asked in 1951 to resign from the Foreign Office.

Mr Philby had been the subject of the closest investigation. No evidence had been found that he was responsible for warning Burgess and Maclean. While in Government service he carried out his duties ably and conscientiously. There was no reason to conclude that he had, at any time, betrayed the interests of Britain, or to identify him with the so-called third man, if there was one.

As regards others whose names had been associated with the affair, he had caused them to be carefully studied and investigated. No one was being shielded. Had any evidence of guilt been forthcoming he, or his predecessors, would not have hesitated to take appropriate action. No such evidence had been found.

A number of Foreign Service officers who had been either office colleagues or had associated outside with Burgess were examined but nothing had been found. If anyone inside or outside the House could produce evidence he trusted it would be made available to the authorities.

Herbert Morrison, MP for Lewisham, South, who had been the Foreign Secretary when the diplomats vanished, said that a newspaper report claimed that Philby and his family had disappeared. Did Mr Macmillan regard that as significant in the circumstances of the case? Mr Macmillan said: 'I have no reason to think they have left this country. I think it is very improbable.'

Melinda Maclean's flight was also raised in the debate, but Mr Macmillan said that Mrs Maclean was of little importance. Anything she knew before Maclean left she must have got from him, and she had no means of obtaining information after he left. Whether she remained in Britain or left made little difference. She could do no good in England and little harm abroad.

There for a time the matter rested. One immediate result was that despite Harold Macmillan's defence of Philby, MI6 finally dismissed him on the grounds that he was now known to have had associations with Burgess. After sharing a house in Washington in 1950 and 1951, this had obviously been known to the authorities all along. Now, however, it was public knowledge, so his suspension on half-pay became the sack.

After a period of odd jobs and unemployment, Philby was hired as the Beirut correspondent of the *Observer* and the *Economist* in 1956. There has been some speculation as to whether, at this stage, he continued to work for MI6. In fact any agents employed in the Secret Service are considered to remain on call even after they have left, and are generally asked to sign an agreement to that effect. It was in that year that Sir Dick White became head of MI6, however, so it is likely that employment of Philby would have been minimal. Sir Dick White had been constant in his certainty that Philby had been working for the KGB. Philby remained in Beirut until early 1963. Significantly, in 1962 the traitor George Blake had been caught. From then on there could not have been the slightest doubt about the role Philby had played as a Soviet agent. Blake had named him.

Philby's life in Beirut was fairly routine. He filed regular and reasonably competent pieces for his Fleet Street employers, and for the rest is remembered largely for the long periods in which he sat alone drinking heavily in his favourite bar. Blake was not the only person to strip Philby of his cover. More and more evidence of his involvement was constantly coming to hand. Towards the end of 1962 it was decided that he should be cross-examined again. The attitude of MI5 and MI6 at this time was that they did not want to prosecute the man but they wanted to know as much as they could about what he had done.

Early in January 1963 a close friend and MI6 colleague of his, Nicholas Elliott, was sent out to Beirut to see if Philby would react favourably to an old-boy approach. Elliott, like Brooman-White, had continued to believe that Philby was innocent; the victim of a chain of circumstantial evidence, the hostility which broke out from time to time between MI5 and MI6 and a friendship for Burgess dating from his days as an undergraduate. Blake's disclosures finally convinced him of the truth.

That Brooman-White and Elliott had found it so hard to accept that Philby was a spy is made easier to understand by R. V. Jones in his book *Most Secret War*. Apart from emphasizing Philby's essential charm, he says: 'So long as the war was on there was a chance that he would survive on Churchill's principle that: "In war you don't have to be polite, you just have to be right!" And Philby had a habit of being right. I think that these characteristics completely prevented any doubts about his ultimate loyalty to the country, if not the various officers in MI6.'

When Elliott arrived in Beirut on January 11th he telephoned Philby immediately saying something like: 'You owe me a drink. Why don't we meet.' Philby, relieved to find a friend in the loneliness of his exile, readily agreed.

When they met, however, his pleasure was short-lived. Elliott did not pull any punches. He made it clear to Philby that he considered that he had breached every code of behaviour and betrayed his personal friendships. Even someone as appallingly self-centred and egotistic as Philby was could not but feel some pangs of guilt.

Elliott is one of the most charming of men. In the bar at White's Club he is the soul of bonhomie – tolerant, even amused, by the failings or eccentricities of his friends. But treachery is something he finds it impossible to forgive. His remorseless examination demonstrated exactly how much was known of Philby's duplicity, and he continually harped on his personal feeling of disgust at the behaviour of someone he had once trusted. Philby started to crack. He realized that he could no longer use the excuse of idealism to salve his conscience for the appalling trail of havoc for which he had been responsible by his selfish pursuit of power. He admitted to Elliott that he had been a spy but said he needed time to think about whether to return to London voluntarily and tell them all he knew. He signed a written confession and Elliott returned to London. There is some evidence that Philby seriously considered returning to face the music, but in the end decided to leave for Russia. He pressed the alarm button and his Russian masters were quick to realize the situation. They must have felt increasing apprehension as his mental state deteriorated and he came increasingly to depend on alcohol. The time had come for him to be removed from the front line. He was in no state to stand up to an MI5 interrogator.

Early on the evening of 23 January 1963 Philby excused himself from an engagement on the grounds that he was tired and that he and his wife were due to dine later with Glen Balfour-Paul, a high-ranking British diplomat. He telephoned his wife to say he might be a little late but would meet her there. He did not keep the appointment, nor was he ever seen again this side of the Iron Curtain. The Russians had put their emergency plan into operation.

His disappearance could not be kept secret for long, of course. On 3 March, his latest wife Eleanor received a cable from Philby postmarked Cairo. On 3 June the Russian paper *Izvestia* reported that the missing man was with the Imam of Yemen. On 1 July 1963, over five months later, the British government announced that Philby was now known to have been a Soviet agent and had indeed been the Third Man.

13 The Fourth Man

It seems likely that if Maclean had travelled to Russia on his own, as was the original intention, Blunt might never have been suspected. Mrs Thatcher's statement says he was interrogated eleven times. He claims that he cannot now remember how often MI5 visited him in his flat. If Burgess had remained in England, the fact that he and Blunt had been meeting would have been easy to explain away and Maclean was not a particular friend of either of them.

There is little doubt that by 1951 Blunt was long out of the spy business. When he had been demobilized after the war he had accepted the highly prestigious post of Director of the Courtauld Institute of Art, where just before the war he had served for a short time as Deputy Director. The Courtauld Institute has a similar role to the Warburg, with which it is on terms of friendly rivalry. Of even more significance, certainly to the general public, was his appointment in 1945, in the reign of King George VI, to be Surveyor of the King's Pictures. He was a trusted member of the Royal Household, and indeed on two occasions immediately after the war he undertook delicate missions on behalf of George VI. The Court were concerned to arrange for the return of certain royal letters known to exist in Germany which, if they got into the wrong hands, might cause considerable embarrassment. They were particularly anxious about letters the Duke of Windsor had written when, shortly after his abdication, he showed every sign of having pro-German sympathies.

By 1951, when Blunt agreed to play his minor role in the escape of Maclean, he must have felt quite safe. Certainly he appeared to have the perfect cover.

It so happened that our book, *Burgess and Maclean*, in which we had pointed the finger in a slightly different direction, had been published only a few weeks before the government named Philby on 1 July 1963. Our candidate for Third Man was Anthony Blunt. Certain papers waded in delightedly claiming that we had been proved wrong. One critic wrote: 'The authors since this book was written before the government's somewhat belated admission about Philby, hint at the identity of the third man, but regrettably events have overtaken them and prove that their guesses are founded on so much gossip. The third man, they say, was a member of MI5. That Philby never was.' But Blunt had been. Our mistake was not to accuse, by implication, an innocent man but to number him Three rather than Four.

Predictably there were others who took the same line. In a greater number of cases, however, reviewers showed serious concern that what we had disclosed was that there were others involved who had not yet been detected. I can remember a critic in the *Daily Telegraph* writing somewhat tetchily: 'If the authors indeed know the identity of the third man, why do they not disclose it?'

In reply, I wrote a letter to the Editor, which was never printed, in which I said I would be happy to do so if he would print it. There was no reply. I was seriously if unnecessarily concerned, however, that by and large everybody seemed to have got it wrong. The original tipoff which led to Maclean's sudden defection was in fact given by Philby to Burgess in Washington. Equally obviously the person most closely concerned that Maclean should get out of the country was Philby, since he feared that Maclean might unmask him under questioning. Nevertheless I was certain that some part must have been played by Blunt and I thought that MI5 might be genuinely unaware of the fact.

After making a few more inquiries I was fairly certain that this was not the case, if only because nobody in MI5 or MI6, many of whom I knew personally, asked me to tell them what I knew or how I came by the knowledge. They must all have known that I knew something and they must also have known that I knew that they knew. Having satisfied myself that the authorities did know about Blunt but had their own reasons for not arresting him, I was quite happy to leave them to play the hand their way and to be thought guilty of picking the wrong man.

Immediately after the government labelled Philby as the Third Man, Marcus Lipton was being heartily slapped on the back for the question he had asked in 1955. Marcus Lipton was above all a good Parliamentarian, and very quick on his feet when it came to asking any sort of question from the castration of cats to the cruelties of battery hen farming. I had the greatest admiration for him. His mild eccentricity concealed a very responsible and caring man.

The *Sunday Times* 'Atticus' column that week was headed 'Mr Lipton of MI7'. It read:

> So large was the gathering of TV and Pressmen at Waterloo Station on Tuesday morning that the rumour went round that *she* was arriving. When the photographers moved forward a hundred onlookers moved with them. Out of the train limped a rather untidy looking man of 62 with a bushy grey moustache, rimless spectacles – and a grin like a Cheshire Cat.
>
> 'The crowd speedily evaporated when they saw it was only me,' said Marcus Lipton, as we sat drinking beer on the House of Commons terrace. 'But I have to admit it was the biggest Press reception I have ever had. Even the Platform foreman, who is a very important person indeed, said "Good morning" to me.'
>
> It was Mr Lipton, of course, who said in the House eight years ago that Philby was the Third Man, but was later made to withdraw it. 'I am feeling rather smugly satisfied,' he said.
>
> Mr Lipton has been Labour MP for Brixton for eighteen years and, along with George Wigg, has become the backbencher most likely to come up with a nasty question . . .
>
> Where does he get all his information?
>
> 'The Philby information came from a contact in the Security Services,' said Lipton. 'I can't possibly give his name. His career would soon be at an end. Philby, of course, is only part of the story. There is no doubt there is still much to be revealed.'

A recent book on Burgess and Maclean suggests that the real 'Third Man' – the one that gave the tip that Maclean was finally to be arrested – was not Philby but a very high official, certainly not a spy, who did it for old-boy reasons. Lipton thinks the theory that the official, now a very high-ranking and well known Establishment figure, is being deliberately concealed may well be true and intends to investigate further.

Immediately I learned that Marcus Lipton was still delving I invited him to lunch and, at risk of deflating his elation at the naming of Philby, I told him the whole story as I knew it and pulled no punches in explaining to him the part that I then thought Anthony Blunt to have played. He had since been knighted, of course, and was very much an Establishment figure, moving in the highest circles.

At first Marcus was incredulous, but after a discussion lasting until the middle afternoon, whilst even the immensely polite waiters were beginning to fidget, I finally convinced him not only that I was right in thinking that Blunt was involved but that it was not in the best interests of the country for him to name him in Parliament as he had named Philby. Finally he said: 'I find what you say completely convincing and I will immediately seek a private meeting with Sir John Hobson.' Hobson was then Attorney General under Harold Macmillan's Prime Ministership and Lord Home's tenure of the Foreign Office. 'I will be guided by him as to what I can best do in the national interests,' he said.

I heard no more of the affair and was happy to think that my conversation, added to the much more weighty arguments of Sir John Hobson, had resulted in silencing Lipton about Blunt's role at that time. I did in fact myself meet Sir John Hobson shortly afterwards and he confirmed that the authorities did indeed believe that the national interest would best be served by discretion. Shortly after this Sir John Hobson authorized the detention of two close Fleet Street colleagues of mine for contempt of Court. Their crime was a very proper refusal to reveal their sources of information. I comforted myself with the thought that it was MI5 and not the Attorney General's office I had decided to support.

The Burgess, Maclean and Philby scandals had been followed by long periods of official silence, then statements which satisfied no one at all. Why when the same situation arose at the end of last year and Sir Anthony Blunt was named in the House of Commons, in the same way that Marcus Lipton had named Philby, was the reaction so entirely different?

For long after the defection of Philby the repercussions had rumbled on.

From time to time another tremor of the earthquake would evince itself. So distinguished an authority as *The Times* suddenly surfaced with an absurd story that the Fourth Man was none other than an amiable old Don at Kings, Cambridge, Donald Beves, who had recently died . . . no libel problems.

The evidence that they produced was based on the rather droll piece of information they had picked up somewhere. The Third or Fourth Man was a Cambridge Don whose name started with the letter 'B' and had five letters. Whoever set that particular *Times* crossword puzzle clue may have known what he was on to. The solver obviously did not. There was no way that anyone with the slightest knowledge of the background of the man could have produced such an improbable solution.

Another writer named another Kings Don, the well-known welfare economist, A. C. Pigou. A keep-fit addict who spent his vacations striding the Cumberland fells, it is hard to imagine anyone more removed from the espionage scene.

Nor do I entirely absolve the erudite Mr Andrew Boyle from starting hares . . . Whilst correctly identifying Anthony Blunt under the code name 'Maurice', he also code-named 'Basil' the man who guided Maclean through the intricacies of atomic espionage whilst the latter had access to CIA files in Washington. But James Angleton managed to detect and 'turn' him after a few months. He afterwards worked for the CIA as a double agent for the next ten years and now, forgiven, lives in happy retirement in the USA . . . 'Basil' may well have existed but he was certainly not Dr Mann, as some newspapers suggested.

Mrs Margaret Thatcher's ready admission of Blunt's involvement was all the more surprising because it has not been denied either by

Blunt or Mrs Thatcher that he had been granted a so-called Queen's Pardon, more correctly described as immunity from prosecution, in 1964.

Mrs Thatcher's statement in answer to a question from Ted Leadbitter, MP, read:

> The name which the Honourable Gentleman has given me is that of Sir Anthony Blunt.
>
> In April 1964, Sir Anthony Blunt admitted to the security authorities that he had been recruited by and had acted as a talent-spotter for Russian intelligence before the war, when he was a don at Cambridge, and had passed information regularly to the Russians while he was a member of the Security Service between 1940 and 1945. He made this admission after being given an undertaking that he would not be prosecuted if he confessed.
>
> Inquiries were, of course, made before Blunt joined the Security Service in 1940, and he was judged a fit person. He was known to have held Marxist views at Cambridge, but the security authorities had no reason either in 1940 or at any time during his service to doubt his loyalty to his country.
>
> On leaving the Security Service in 1945 Blunt reverted to his profession as an art historian. He held a number of academic appointments. He was also appointed as Surveyor of the King's Pictures in 1945, and as Surveyor of the Queen's Pictures in 1952. He was made a KCVO in 1956. On his retirement as Surveyor, he was appointed as an Adviser for the Queen's Pictures and Drawings in 1972, and he retired from this appointment in 1978.
>
> He first came under suspicion in the course of the inquiries which followed the defection of Burgess and Maclean in 1951, when the Security Service was told that Burgess had said in 1937 that he was working for a secret branch of the Comintern and that Blunt was one of his sources. There was no supporting evidence for this. When confronted with it Blunt denied it.
>
> Nevertheless the Security Service remained suspicious of

him, and began an intensive and prolonged investigation of his activities. During the course of this investigation he was interviewed on 11 occasions. He persisted in his denial, and no evidence against him was obtained.

The inquiries which preceded the exposure and defection of Philby in January, 1963, produced nothing which implicated Blunt. Early in 1964, new information was received which directly implicated Blunt. It did not, however, provide a basis on which charges could be brought. The then Attorney General decided in April, 1964, after consultation with the Director of Public Prosecutions, that the public interest lay in trying to secure a confession from Blunt, not only to arrive at a definite conclusion on his own involvement but also to obtain information from him about any others who might still be a danger.

It was considered important to gain his cooperation in the continuing investigations by the security authorities, following the defections of Burgess, Maclean and Philby, into Soviet penetration of the Security and Intelligence Services and other public services during and after the war. Accordingly the Attorney General authorized the offer of immunity from prosecution to Blunt if he confessed.

Blunt then admitted to the security authorities that, like his friends Burgess, Maclean and Philby, he had become an agent of Russian intelligence and had talent-spotted for them at Cambridge during the 1930s; that he had regularly passed information to the Russians while he was a member of the Security Services; and that, although after 1945 he was no longer in a position to supply the Russians with classified information, in 1951 he used his old contact with the Russian Intelligence Service to assist in the arrangements for the defection of Burgess and Maclean.

Both at the time of his confession and subsequently Blunt provided useful information about Russian intelligence activities and about his association with Burgess, Maclean and Philby.

The Queen's Private Secretary was informed in April, 1964, both of Blunt's confession and of the immunity from prosecution on the basis of which it had been made. Blunt was not required to resign his appointment in the Royal Household, which was unpaid. It carried with it no access to classified information and no risk to security, and the security authorities thought it desirable not to put at risk his cooperation.

The decision to offer immunity from prosecution was taken because intensive investigation from 1951 to 1964 had produced no evidence to support charges. Successive Attorneys General in 1973, in June, 1974, and in June, 1979, have agreed that, having regard to the immunity granted in order to obtain the confession, which has always been and still is the only firm evidence against Blunt, there are no grounds on which criminal proceedings could be instituted.

That this statement should be regarded by some as a welcome breath of fresh air, in an area where there have been palpable cover-ups over many years, is not a view that I share. The whole statement is reminiscent of the much criticized Government White Paper published three and a half years after the Burgess and Maclean incident.

To say for example that 'inquiries were made before Blunt joined the Security Service and he was judged a fit person' only raises further questions. If he was judged a fit person in 1940 why was he chucked out of the Intelligence School at Minley Manor almost within hours of being enrolled for the course in 1939? If two investigative journalists like Purdy and me found it so easy to discover that he had been involved, through his Russian contacts, in assisting in the escape of Burgess and Maclean, I cannot imagine that no one in the serried ranks of our Secret Service, with the advantage of access to much more information than we had, had not come up with the same answer.

Nor can I believe that frequent interrogations of Blunt over a period of several years, if really vigorously carried out, would have failed to break him. My own brief meeting with him in the Travellers' Club in 1962 was enough to convince me that he was not cast in a heroic mould. Indeed, it was reported in the Press on the following day that he had had a mild heart attack.

If my 1963 revelations could be airily dismissed as 'mere gossip', by their own admission the Security Services were in full possession of the facts in 1964 – fifteen years ago. That Blunt was allowed to remain in a high position of trust, even spending weekends with the Royal Family at Windsor, must be sufficient proof that by then, if not much earlier, he had been completely defused. This makes the revelations following the publication of Andrew Boyle's book, *The Climate of Treason*, even more difficult to understand.

Mrs Thatcher must certainly have known that she was about to explode a bomb whose reverberations would be far greater than anything which had gone before.

The public interest in Burgess, Maclean and Philby stems largely from their upper-class backgrounds. The continued interest in them has driven spies of far greater importance into obscurity.

That the naming of Sir Anthony Blunt would cause an explosion of public indignation was completely predictable. Here is the entry under his name in the 1979 edition of *Who's Who*.

BLUNT, Sir Anthony Frederick, KCVO 1956 (CVO 1947); FBA 1950; FSA 1960; Professor of History of Art, University of London, and Director, Courtauld Institute of Art, 1947–September 1974; Surveyor of the Queen's Pictures, 1952–72 (of the Pictures of King George VI, 1945–52); Adviser for the Queen's Pictures and Drawings, since 1972; b. 26 September 1907, y.s. of late Rev. A. S. V. Blunt, Vicar of St John's Paddington. *Educ*: Marlborough Coll., Trinity Coll., Cambridge. Served War of 1939–45: France 1939–40, War Office 1940–45. Fellow, Trinity Coll., Cambridge, 1932–36; on staff of Warburg Institute, London, 1937–39; Reader in History of Art, London University, and Deputy Director, Courtauld Institute of Art 1939–47. Slade Prof. of Fine Art, Oxford, 1962–63; Cambridge, 1965–66. Hon. Fellow, Trinity Coll., Cambridge 1967. Hon. FRIBA, 1973, Hon. DLitt: Bristol 1961; Durham, 1963; Oxon., 1971; DèsL hc Paris, 1966. Commander Order of Orange Nassau (Holland) 1948; Legion of Honour (France), 1958. *Publications*: (with Walter Friedlaender) The Drawings of Nicolas Poussin,

1939–75; Artistic Theory in Italy, 1940; François Mansart, 1941; French Drawings at Windsor Castle, 1945; (with Margaret Whinney) The Nation's Pictures, 1951; Rouault's Miserere, 1951; Poussin's Golden Calf, 1951; Art and Architecture in France, 1500–1700, 1953, rev. edn. 1970; The Drawings of G. B. Castiglione and Stefano della Bella at Windsor Castle, 1954; Venetian Drawings at Windsor Castle, 1957; Philibert de l'Orme, 1958; The Art of William Blake, 1960; (with H. L. Cooke) The Roman Drawings at Windsor Castle, 1960; (with Phoebe Pool) Picasso: The Formative Years, 1962; Nicolas Poussin: Catalogue raisonné, 1966; Nicolas Poussin (2 vols), 1967; Sicilian Baroque, 1968; Picasso's Guernica, 1969; Supplement to Italian and French Drawings at Windsor, 1971; Neapolitan Baroque and Rococo Architecture, 1975; articles in Burlington Magazine, Jl of Warburg and Courtauld Insts., Spectator, etc. Address: 45 Portsea Hall, Portsea Place, W.2. Club: Travellers'.

Because of this record, the popular Press leapt in with wild headlines like 'Spy in the Palace'. Anti-Royalist MPs like Willie Hamilton and others did their best to turn it into some sort of political issue. Even the staider papers had a field day. The *Sunday Telegraph* came out with an infamous article declaring that Captain Anthony Blunt had sent many gallant members of the SOE to their deaths in occupied Holland. In fact the most cursory check would have revealed that Blunt never was a member of the SOE. Anyway what would a dedicated communist have been doing assisting the hated Nazis? This monstrous allegation merited a minute, tucked away, apology the following Sunday.

The inevitable witch hunt, trying to discover more candidates for burning, reached a point of hysteria not even achieved in the religious persecutions of the fifteenth and sixteenth centuries. Names were tossed around like confetti. Victor Rothschild's friendship with Burgess at Cambridge and during the war became a matter for open speculation. Sir Fred Warner, who had shared an office with Burgess so many years ago; Roger Makins, now Lord Sherfield, who had been Maclean's boss at the Foreign Office at the time of his defection; even Peter Wilson, the highly respected Chairman of Sotheby's, whose retirement happened to coincide with the Blunt disclosures and who was thought to have served in one of the Secret Services during the war . . . all were thrown into the Fleet Street boiling pot for good luck.

In the midst of all the wild accusations and professions of outrage, nobody bothered to ask the right questions.

The really important question was just how guilty Blunt had been. To read the Press reports it would appear that he had masterminded the whole affair and spirited two traitors into the hands of the Russians from under the very nose of MI5.

Of course this is palpable nonsense. Blunt had neither the resources nor the muscle to do anything of the sort. As we have seen, Philby was the main instigator and Burgess the willing helper. The fact that Burgess himself was in no position to activate the Russians demonstrates just how unimportant he was. The extent of Blunt's intervention was possibly a matter of just one telephone call.

One of the reasons why I accepted in 1962 that to try to add to the battle scars MI5 had already collected over the whole affair was unjustified was that I was not at all sure that, in their anxiety to get rid of Maclean without having to bring him to trial, it might not have been our own people who called Blunt in from the cold and asked him for his cooperation. If this had been so, of course, his action would have been one of loyalty rather than treason.

I am now satisfied that this was not the case. But the spate of current rumours that the late Guy Liddell, deputy head of MI5, was guiltily involved is utterly ridiculous.

Like most ordinary people, I react angrily to the evidence that one of my fellow-countrymen has acted traitorously. I do not make any plea in mitigation of judgement on any of the four I have written about. My only hope is that the preceding pages will go some way to abating the spy fever which seems to afflict us with such monotonous regularity.

Undoubtedly, however, there will be one or two long dead moles who will be dug out of holes from time to time by assiduous investigators. Further public outrage will erupt at what has become known to the public, somewhat romantically, as The Great Cambridge Communist Conspiracy.

The latest victim of this passion for exposing suspects the extent of whose guilt has long been known to our Security Services is the sixty-six-year-old John Cairncross. I find the triumphant production of names like these by newspaper investigators as amusing as watching a stage magician producing the traditional rabbit out of a hat. Given a little training anyone can do it.

Here is the formula. Look down the list of Cambridge undergraduates in the 1930s with particular attention to Trinity College or Trinity Hall. Trace any evidence of expressed communist sympathies, any evidence of membership of the Apostles or any known homosexual deviationism. Evidence of one or more of these qualifications and, Hey-presto!, you have a suspect. Prove postgraduate association with any of the names like Blunt, Philby, Burgess or Maclean, and the suspicion deepens. Look up any reference book and discover that they have had subsequent careers in the Foreign Office or a wartime career which is so vaguely described as to make it likely that they served in one of the Secret Services, and you are possibly on to a winner ... or possibly not. It is a game anyone can play. If your suspect is dead so much the better.

John Cairncross, like several others, fitted part of the formula. Now he has admitted that he did pass odd pieces of information to his gossip-hungry friend, Guy Burgess. He had passed the Foreign Office examination with brilliance, and repeated some chit-chat he had had with Sir John Colville, later to become Secretary to Sir Winston Churchill, but then a Foreign Office colleague. The information was divulged at 'a casual and friendly lunch'. The nature of the gossip could hardly have been world-shaking, but undoubtedly John Cairncross, who shortly afterwards shed his earlier communist ideals and went on to a distinguished career in the Treasury, felt some guilt about the matter. After the flight of Burgess he began to think that his erstwhile friend might have been more important in relation to the KGB than he had suspected – or indeed, than he actually was. His feeling of guilt may have been all the more marked because his even more distinguished brother was to be knighted for his services as economic adviser to the government.

It can be only to the credit of MI5 that, following the defection of Burgess in 1951, Cairncross was one among many of Burgess's former associates who was picked up for questioning by such experts in the business as William Skardon, to whom he admitted the exact extent of his involvement. He resigned from public life without a pension, went to live abroad, and that was the end of that.

The riveting revelations about him in a Sunday newspaper in December 1979, trying to make a big story out of a non-event, were lent poignancy by the statement that they had promised not to reveal the present whereabouts of Mr Cairncross. Of course anybody who wished to know could find out quite easily that since his retirement he has lived in Rome. There was never any secret about the fact.

In a dignified letter to *The Times*, Mrs Hector McNeil expressed her distress that, since her husband's death in 1955 his reputation had been continually libelled. Andrew Boyle attributed his heart attack to guilt and remorse . . . I have every sympathy for her. Why should McNeil have felt guilty that he liked Burgess and believed in his abilities? Until 1951 his opinions were shared by many Establishment figures. Betrayed he may have felt but surely not guilty or remorseful. The so-called death bed revelations of my old friend Goronwy Rees have also been given an airing to prove the guilt of others already dead. Such allegations are often untrue and do the authors no credit.

As it has now been admitted that Blunt was called in for questioning in 1951, it raises the whole matter of why it is claimed that in 1964 he was granted immunity from prosecution in return for a full confession.

A full confession of what? His wartime activities? His communism at Cambridge? The part he played in the Burgess and Maclean affair? Surely not. But what else could he possibly confess to so belatedly after at least thirteen years of interrogation? The answer is nothing.

I am satisfied that MI5 knew everything they wanted to know by 1951 and a decision was then taken to brush it under the carpet. Blunt was already an established figure and could do no further harm, so why rub salt into an already very painful wound? By 1964, however, so many people knew of his involvement, partly perhaps because of the book Purdy and I had written, that the authorities decided that it was necessary to give him (and themselves) active protection.

Perhaps, too, when his name was tabled in the House of Commons in 1979, Mrs Thatcher decided that further dissimulation was impossible. This way her action makes some sort of sense.

The spy hysteria which followed illustrates two points: it shows that Anthony Blunt's statement that all the 'Cambridge ring' of the 1930s had been defused can be believed, and it demonstrates that the professionals were far ahead of the amateurs after the defections of 1951. Blunt's association with Burgess and the rest must have been known and regarded as of much greater importance than that of the latest Press 'discovery', Mr Cairncross.

Nevertheless, the ridiculousness of throwing members of the Cambridge Connection or other associates of the four men to the lions should not lend credence to the belief that there is no further danger to our security. MI5 remain diligent in the rather unglamorous field of counter-espionage, and should be encouraged to do so.

14 The Old Boys' Reunion

This book is an attempt to put into perspective the relative importance of all the *dramatis personae* involved. I hope I have shown that the circumstances and the timing of the unmasking of Andrew Boyle's 'Maurice' as Sir Anthony Blunt, by the immense disproportion of the publicity it was accorded, has thrown the whole long story completely out of balance. The colourfulness of Burgess, the conservative-front bohemianism of Maclean, the cold-blooded calculations of Philby, and finally the homosexual and intellectual motivation of Blunt make a fascinating study of contrasting motives, ambitions and weaknesses.

Today Blunt alone is left in this country, his reputation in ruins. Stripped of all his honours, he has been left only with the loyalties of his colleagues and his students, whose reaction to his sudden disgrace may be summed up as: 'It is impossible to believe. He was a man of such immense academic brilliance, kindness and personal charm.' Perhaps, too, there must be some tinge of sadness amongst those, like myself, who do not know him well, that those who rushed to heap honours upon him should have so denied him in his hour of need. Yet that may be dismissed as pure sentimentality, for he was without doubt a traitor to the very society which has acclaimed him.

But what of the others?

Burgess, not because of his moral scruples but because of his indiscretion, was the least effective active agent of them all. He was the one, predictably, who got the shortest shrift when, to their mutual embarrassment, he found himself the unwanted guest of the Soviet Union.

Jim Andreyevitch Eliot, to give him his Russian pseudonym, never really recovered from the transplant operation which replaced his hedonistic enjoyment of the good things of life and the freedom to criticize it, with the necessity of coming to terms with the harsh realities of existence under the regime whose ideals he had so mischievously propagated. He did more damage to the communist cause he sought to disseminate by defecting than he ever did to assist it in the years before. Apart from compromising Philby and Blunt his compulsive habit of making notes about everyone of the slightest possible interest with whom he came in contact during his career led to a number of quiet dismissals within the Establishment. With typical untidiness many of his random jottings were discovered after he had left and led to identifying many (perhaps twenty) politically suspect names.

His final years in Moscow, discredited, and ever-itching in the hair-shirt of the exile to which he had condemned himself, were squalid and pathetic.

When he came to die his lonely death on 19 August 1963 at the Bodkin Hospital in Moscow with only Tolya, his boyfriend, by his side there were many who had deplored his way of life but who sorrowed at the manner of his leaving it.

As for Maclean, after they had arrived together in Moscow his career diverged from Burgess's in the same way that their careers had diverged since those first heady days up at Cambridge.

At first, whilst they were being kept 'under wraps', they were immured outside Moscow, well concealed in the anonymity of a small industrial town. They shared a worker's apartment which, at least for Burgess, was the equivalent of being moved from a luxury flat in Mayfair to a council flat in Crewe.

In his assessment of the two men, Herbert Morrison, Foreign Secretary at the time of their flight, wrote these impressions of them, gathered from others (he himself had never met either):

> Burgess was the more lively and potentially dangerous partner. I did not meet him, so far as I recall. I gathered that

he was an intelligent and rather bumptious young man – a typical career diplomat. As personal assistant to the Minister of State, Hector McNeil, he had access to the documents. McNeil liked him, regarded him as a live wire, with a pleasant manner and considerable intelligence; indeed he had pressed for Burgess as his personal assistant.

It is strange, therefore, that the security authorities regarded Maclean as the principal suspect. He was, as a result of his Cairo breakdown, less highly regarded.

A more inept summing up of the personalities or relative importance of the two men would have been hard to imagine.

If Herbert Morrison was misinformed about the relative importance of the two men, the KGB were certainly not.

After their joint stay outside Moscow whilst the first stage of their lengthy debriefing was in progress, they were both given jobs in the vastly complex and powerful body euphoniously known as the State Publishing House. Briefly they both enjoyed the same evidence of official regard – dachas in the country, priority tickets for the Bolshoi, official motor cars. But as the relative importance of the two men became ever more evident, so did their paths start to diverge. Burgess headed downwards even to the extent that the Soviet authorities suspected, at one stage, that he might well have been planted by the British as an undercover agent, and had his dacha bugged. Maclean, meanwhile, rose higher and higher in official esteem.

By the time that Melinda joined Maclean with the children his position was secure, whilst Burgess became more and more of an embarrassment to his increasingly reluctant hosts. But it was only when Kim Philby qualified for his old-boy tie and arrived in Moscow that the relative unimportance of the other two became apparent.

Philby was to be joined by his third wife Eleanor nine months later, in a reunion actively assisted by the British, and right from the very beginning their life together in Moscow was one of privilege. The debriefing of Philby was of such importance that it took over two years before it was painstakingly completed.

The event was marked in 1965 by the award of the Soviet Union's 'Red Banner of Honour', one of the highest orders that could be bestowed for services to the country. He was given the rank of colonel in the KGB.

The relationship between the Philbys in their exile was not necessarily an easy one. Eleanor Philby found Kim difficult and moody. He was prone to long periods of heavy drinking, interrupted by weeks of high elation as his affairs prospered with his new employers. There were constant rows about such important issues as his heavy drinking and such relatively minor matters as the care of the caged birds with which he filled their Moscow flat.

Philby's personal problems did not end with drink or his relationship with his masters. During all his career, in the course of which he had married three times, he had had a constant succession of mistresses. In Moscow such extramarital activities were seriously curtailed.

In her autobiography Eleanor recalls that evenings spent together with the Macleans were often climaxed by reading Purdy's and my book *Burgess and Maclean*, and when it came to our account of Melinda's own flight she would burst into floods of sentimental tears. The friendship between the two families, always slightly artificial, suffered a severe setback when the egregious Philby persuaded Melinda to desert Donald and move in with him. Brokenhearted, Eleanor returned to America in 1965, and died there three years later.

As neither Philby nor Maclean mix with the British Press contingent in Moscow, as Guy Burgess used to do, not much is known about their lives – nor, indeed, is there any reason why the country they betrayed should continue to be interested in them.

Melinda Maclean failed to keep the fickle Philby's interest alive for long. He may or may not have gone through a form of marriage with her after his third wife, Eleanor, died and she certainly shared his flat for a time. By 1970 he had left her for a Russian girl called Nina and they certainly claim to be married. Perhaps by the time this book is published he will have got tired of Nina and remarried for the fourth, fifth or sixth time.

Despite his drinking and his apparently disorganized private life, however, Philby remains the good civil servant he has always been. He can be seen on every working day reporting punctually to his office at KGB Headquarters. No doubt he is as good at his job and as popular with his colleagues as he was in MI6. At any rate, sometime in 1978 he was promoted to the rank of general.

Donald Maclean took Melinda back in 1970 after Philby had finished with her. Melinda went to America in 1976 to visit her relations and many people expected her to stay there for good. She was back with Donald in Moscow after a few months, however, and seems to be there still. Presumably both the Macleans, like Philby, have adapted to life in Russia as Burgess never could.

15 What Did They Do For Russia?

Anthony Blunt's role is, perhaps, the most difficult to assess in 1980. In the first place he was only publicly exposed on 15 November 1979. So far very few of the people who might talk about him have had time to give considered thought to the far-off days when he was an active Soviet agent. Second, he has made a not entirely reliable statement; answered various questions; avoided others by pleading the Official Secrets Act and now promises to write his own book. Lastly, he is a man of seventy-two and when he says that he cannot remember whether he first agreed to work for the Russians in 1935 or 1936 I have little difficulty in believing him. What seems fairly well established, however, is that between 1936 and 1939 he used his position as a Don at Trinity to search out likely prospects for Russian employment. Presumably he gave MI5 a complete list of his recruits in 1964, and any who *were* still active must have been neutralized then.

During his brief period as an active soldier Captain Blunt can have had nothing of interest to transmit to his masters. When he joined MI5 later in 1940, however, things changed. He claims that he told them about the running and staffing of the organization and later about German Intelligence networks. Some people have claimed that, until the German invasion of Russia, this information might have been passed back to the Nazis and proved invaluable to them. I think this most unlikely. When the Russians became our Allies, they could probably have got whatever information we had about German Intelligence by asking for it through diplomatic channels. Perhaps they did, but because Stalin's was a suspicious

WHAT DID THEY DO FOR RUSSIA?

nature, decided to keep Blunt working away in secret as a check on what they were getting officially.

There remains the question of the Allied governments in exile in London. Blunt seems to have had access to MI5 information about them. Mrs Thatcher has said in Parliament that, so far as is known, Blunt was not responsible for the death of any British agents. But what of, for instance, the Czechs? While the *Sunday Telegraph* allegation that he was responsible for the tragic SOE blunder in Holland is totally untrue, there is no certainty that his treachery did not cost Allied lives between 1940 and 1945.

After he left MI5 at the end of the war, Anthony Blunt seems only to have been called upon to do two minor chores. In 1951 Guy Burgess asked him to get the Russians to arrange Maclean's escape. He could have made a better job of it. But perhaps there are circumstances, still unknown, which account for the fact that Burgess left with him leaving a trail across Europe which a Boy Scout could have followed. And, of course, Burgess's departure compromised not only Blunt himself but Philby as well. The last task that he is generally known to have performed was to get in touch with Philby in 1954 or 1955 and re-establish his contact with the Russians.

In 1964 he made a full confession to MI5. Let us hope that it was useful to them after the monstrously long time he made them wait for it.

Kim Philby is probably the most successful spy ever to have existed outside the pages of a novel. Not only did he work for the Russians on and off from 1934 until 1963 but he organized the department of MI6 specially created to spy on his employers.

His work for the communist underground in Vienna in 1934 was his baptism of fire. He claims in his autobiography that his Soviet mentors spent the years from then until 1940 carefully and patiently training him in espionage techniques and that he was ashamed and humiliated that he had so little information to give them.

In June 1940 he joined an SOE training section and, later that year, was transferred to MI6. In 1941 he was in their Iberian subsection; in 1942 he was put in charge of North Africa and Italy as well as Spain and Portugal. But, according to his own account, he always had easy access to any file that he wanted to consult. There is little doubt that not much information was gathered by MI6 about any country in the world between mid-1940 and 1944 that Philby did not pass to Moscow.

Perhaps 1944 was his year of greatest triumph. MI6 decided to create a new department to spy on their former Allies, the Russians, and their communist supporters on both sides of the Iron Curtain. Their choice to recruit for and set up the new section was Kim Philby. According to Graham Greene he set about the task with his usual energy and efficiency and made an excellent job of it. The advantage to the Russians of having the network designed to spy on them and their friends organized and run by an agent of theirs of ten years' standing is almost impossible to envisage.

In 1945 Philby was nearly unmasked when Volkov, an employee of a Russian Consulate in Turkey, offered to name Soviet spies in England in return for political asylum. Of course, as MI6's Soviet expert, Philby was chosen to go and collect him. Equally naturally, in the circumstances, when Philby arrived in Istanbul, Volkov had mysteriously vanished never to be heard of again. By this time the anti-Soviet section of MI6 was so well run that people were talking of Philby as a likely future head of the whole organization. He needed to broaden his experience.

From 1946 to 1949 Philby ran the MI6 station in Turkey. His colleagues agree that he ran it magnificently. Never had the Turkish section done such good work: never, presumably, had the Russians been so meticulously informed of their every move.

In 1949 Philby was promoted and sent to Washington, ostensibly as a First Secretary in the British Embassy but in fact as the chief MI6 officer in charge of a large section that worked with the CIA and the FBI. Another plum job for Philby. The Russians already knew all there was to know about MI6; now they could find out a lot of useful details about their American opposite numbers. But sometime in Philby's years in Washington, James Angleton of the CIA became suspicious of Philby and probably the KGB told him to lie low. Philby's book gives little useful information and he does not admit that there was ever a time when the Russians were not in constant touch with him. I believe, however, that by late 1950 or early 1951 he was on the Russians' 'temporarily inactive' list.

In May 1951 the flight of Burgess and Maclean proved to be a blow from which Philby's brilliant career never recovered. He was recalled to London immediately after their departure and interrogated intermittently while holding down a series of boring jobs until he went to Beirut as a journalist in 1956 and fled from there to Moscow in 1963. It is unlikely that he was of much use to the Russians after the spring of 1951. There is no doubt that he has many lives, British, Allied and Russian, on his conscience.

The high point of Guy Burgess's career as a Soviet agent would seem to have been in the mid-Thirties. He recruited Anthony Blunt and possibly Donald Maclean as well. No doubt there were many others but, as his attempt to enlist the services of Goronwy Rees shows, his judgement as to who was ripe for treason was not always good.

No doubt he did useful courier jobs, like taking money and messages to Philby in Spain and informing his contacts of the state of French morale as he judged it through his contacts with Daladier's office, but there is little evidence that he was ever employed by the Russians on a regular basis and much to suggest that he was not. I doubt whether he ever had a regular letter drop or photographed a secret document in his life.

His role, if he really had one, during his years in the Foreign Office, would have been to give background assessments of high policy from time to time and to do what he could to persuade friends and colleagues that Britain's anti-Soviet policy was misconceived and the Americans not to be trusted. In fact, for all his bombast and apparent unreliability, Guy was extremely shrewd and his views on the power structure in the Foreign Office and the Labour or Conservative governments, as they affected Anglo-Russian relations, are likely to have been well worth taking seriously. I doubt whether the Russians would have appreciated the fact. He told Tom Driberg a lot about his treatment in Russia in his early years which did not, for obvious reasons, appear in print. One of his complaints was that they were more inclined to believe Donald Maclean or even the *Times* leader writers than him. He also maintained to Driberg and to friends he wrote to in later years that the Russians did not want him, that he had never 'really' been a spy, that he had no hope of getting an interesting job in Moscow and that he could not imagine why he could not return to England.

The exact moment when Donald Maclean was recruited as a Comintern agent or whether it was Burgess, Blunt or someone quite different who signed him on is difficult to discover. It seems quite certain, however, that sometime in 1934 or 1935 he was persuaded that openly communist affiliations and a career as a teacher in Russia would be of less use to the Soviets in the long run than a successful career in the Foreign Service.

My guess is that he was a 'mole', perfecting his conventional cover, from 1936 to 1944 when he went to the Embassy in Washington. There he was activated and undoubtedly passed to the Russians regularly all that he knew. Until recently I had imagined that in those four years he must have been in a position to do nearly as much harm to Britain and considerably more to America than even Kim Philby. This was mainly because he became Secretary to the Anglo-American committee on the future use of the newly tested atomic weapon in the summer of 1945 and had a pass to the Atomic Energy Commission in Washington. If one accepts Andrew Boyle's theory that the CIA 'turned' a KGB agent who advised him on what documents to copy after a few months, the picture brightens. It is a fact, nevertheless, that in order to run a double agent and feed disinformation to a foreign power, one has to allow through a great deal of real information one would rather keep to oneself. A failure to do so immediately arouses suspicion and the operation comes to an end. In this situation, therefore, a realistic assessment of the harm done by Maclean is virtually impossible. What seems quite certain is that he himself never had an inkling that his adviser was working for the CIA. If 'Basil' did exist and was a double agent, Andrew Boyle's book must have come as a nasty shock to him as to Anthony Blunt.

By the time he was transferred to Cairo the Russians may have been having doubts about whether the stuff he had been sending them from America was all that accurate and useful. It is not likely, therefore, that they made use of him either during his Cairo posting or after he returned to London. This sudden withdrawal of Soviet support may account both for his drinking suddenly getting out of hand and for the fact that the KGB seem to have treated him with some suspicion when he first arrived in Moscow.

Could it happen again? I suppose so. The climate of the Thirties with a weak British government in charge of a far-flung Empire and of whom much was expected; the Spanish civil war which made so many feel that Right was wrong and Left was right; the alarmingly rapid rise of the peculiarly horrible Hitler ... I can think of no historical parallels and devoutly hope that that particular concatenation of circumstances will not arise again.

It must also be taken into account that the four young converts to communism were exceptional. Blunt, the only one whose career continued into middle age, is a renowned art historian with an internationally recognized reputation. Philby would almost certainly have become head of MI6 and Maclean Permanent Under Secretary at the Foreign Office in due course. Burgess probably had too little application and discipline for a high position in the Establishment, but he would have been an eccentric who knew everybody and was respected for his genuine kindness and wit in social circles, and in academic circles for his remarkably quick and original mind.

Obviously all four had character defects – they would not have been traitors otherwise. But the fact that all four had exceptional qualities as well does make it easier to understand how and why they remained unsuspected for so long. Everyone can imagine the envious, embittered, second-raters taking to espionage (or embezzlement, for that matter) but these were not second-rate men.

The Establishment cover-up so dear to the readers of the popular Press simply did not happen. No one, with the exception of a few security officials, suspected Maclean before his flight; no one, so far as I know, ever suspected Burgess at all. In the twelve long years between the departure of the first two and his own defection some of Philby's friends and colleagues thought he was the victim of a witch hunt and guilty of little worse than having failed to spot Burgess as a KGB agent. No doubt London is teeming with people, wise after the event, who always suspected Blunt. Anthony Purdy and I took quite a lot of convincing in 1962 and we tended to be treated as lunatics if we aired our knowledge of his guilt to anyone who knew him.

However, there will no doubt be other times and other climates in which a closely-knit fraternity of spies can flourish. Indeed there can be little doubt that all the Great Powers, and many more minor ones, are busily engaged at this moment in trying to create just such climates. In my opinion it would be utterly idiotic for them not to do so.

After all, espionage is the second oldest profession in the world.

Index

Acheson, Dean, 78
Acol Road, 37
Albania, plot concerning, 88-9, 128
Alison, Barley, 73, 128
Alsop, Joe, 92
Amies, Hardy, 69
Angleton, James, 136, 147, 164
Anglo-German Fellowship, 51
Anti-War Movement, 45
Apostles, Society of the, 46
Armstrong, Sir Robert, 17
Attlee, Clement, 28
Auden, W. H., 100, 123

Baddeley, Hermione, 75
Balfour-Paul, Glen, 142
Bartlett, Vernon, 51
'Basil', 98-9, 147
Basset, Colonel John Retallack, 38
Beaconshaw, 85
Beauvallon, 111
Beaverbrook, Lord, 134-5
'Becker, Robert', 121
Bell, Julian, 41
Berry, Michael (later Lord Hartwell), 94
Beves, Donald, 147
Birley, Robert, 39

Blackburn, Raymond, 23
Blaikie, Derek, 72
Blake, George, 26, 140
Blundell, Sir Robert, 129
Blunt, Rev. A. S. V. (father of Anthony), 34, 36
Blunt, Anthony
  as art historian, 35, 48, 50, 143, 148, 167
  his birth, parents, schooling, 34-5
  Burgess a close friend, 35, 41, 43, 46, 48, 95-6
  Burgess shares flat with, 18, 95
  at Cambridge, 33, 35, 40
  his communist sympathies, 27, 35, 48-9, 67-8
  at Courtauld Institute, 50, 143
  and flight of Maclean and Burgess, 17-18, 94-5, 101-2, 106-8 143-9, 153, 163
  his homosexuality, 35, 47
  in Intelligence Corps, 65-7
  in MI5, 67, 68, 88, 162-3
  not put on trial, 25
  as spy, Russian agent, 26, 27, 29, 33-4, 48, 54, 68 *passim*, 162-3, 147-56
  suspected, possibly, 167
  today, 157

Blunt, Anthony—*cont.*
  'upper-class', 22
  at Warburg Institute, 48, 50
  in *Who's Who*, 151–2
Blunt, Wilfred (brother of
  Anthony), 34
Boyle, Andrew, 17–18, 19, 20, 24,
  73, 98, 99, 147, 151, 156 166
Boyle, Ed, 17–18
Brooman-White, Dick, 137, 141
Bukharin, Nikolai, 52
Bulganin, Nikolai, 125–6
Burgess, Evelyn (*née* Gillman;
  mother of Guy), 38, 106
Burgess, Guy Francis de Moncy
  at the BBC, 54, 60–1, 67, 70
  his birth, family, childhood,
    schooling, 38–9
  Blunt a close friend, 35, 41, 43,
    46, 48, 95–6
  Blunt shares a flat with, 18, 95
  at Cambridge, 33, 39, 43–7
  and Churchill, 55
  his communist sympathies, 45,
    47, 48, 52, 53–4, 57
  and Daladier, 58–9
  his death, 158
  his domestic arrangements, 55–6
  Driberg's biography of, 19, 127–8
  his drinking, 72, 74–5, 90, 92
  his flight with Maclean, 18, 30,
    94–9, 100–9, 119–28, 129–34, 144,
    149, 163
  in Foreign Office, 71–6, 89–93,
    98–9, 128
  his homosexuality, 44, 47, 56, 68,
    90, 92
  and Colonel Macnamara, MP,
    53
  Moscow life of, 158–9
  never suspected, 156, 167
  not put on trial, 25
  his personality, 20, 43, 46–7, 59,
    60, 92–3, 167
  his postgraduate year, 52–3
  and von Putlitz, 57
  and Mrs Rothschild, 52–3, 57–8
  and Section D, 61, 64
  and SOE, 67
  as spy, Russian agent, 19, 26–7, 45,
    47, 52, 53–4, 58–60, 157–8, 165
  and John Strachey, 67–8
  at *The Times*, 52
  'upper-class', 22
  mentioned, 68
Burgess, Malcolm (father of Guy),
  38
Burgess, Nigel (brother of Guy),
  38

Cairncross, John, 154–6
Cambridge University
  communism at, 43, 48
  see also Pembroke College;
    Trinity College; Trinity Hall
Carey-Foster, G. A., 105, 108–9
Chamberlain, Neville, 45, 58
Chance, Sir Roger, 51
Churchill, Sir Winston, 23, 55
Colville, Sir John, 154
communism, pre-war sympathy for,
  33, 35, 43, 47–8
Connolly, Cyril, 46, 96–7
Cornford, John, 41, 48
Courtauld Institute of Art, 50, 143
Crossman, Richard, 138
Culme-Seymour, Mark, 62, 96
Curry, George, 66

Daladier, Édouard, 57, 58, 59

INDEX

Dehn, Paul, 69
Deighton, Len, 21
Delmer, Sefton, 57
Dobbs, F. W., 39
Domville, Admiral Barry, 33, 53
Driberg, Tom, 19, 44, 46, 47, 58 91, 127-8, 165
Dunbar, Mrs (mother of Melinda Maclean), 62, 84, 105, 111-18, *passim*, 121

Eden, Anthony, 90-1, 134
Edinburgh, Duke of, 80
Elliott, Nicholas, 141-2
Elphick, Robert, 130
Eton College, 22, 39

Fleming, Ian, 24
Franco, General, 51
Franks, Sir Oliver, 92
Fuchs, Klaus, 25, 78

Gargoyle Club, 75, 86
George VI, King, 143
Gillman, Evelyn, *see* Burgess, Evelyn
Gimpel, René, 35
Gladwyn, Lord, *see* Jebb, Sir Gladwyn
Grand, Colonel Laurence Douglas, 61, 64-5
Graves, Sir Cecil, 54
Greene, Graham, 21, 164
Gresham's School, 22, 40
Gubbins, Colin, 67, 68

Haden-Guest, David, 41
Hamilton, Willie, 152
Harper, Stephen, 133
Harris, Tómas and Hilda, 69

Hartwell, Lord, *see* Berry, Michael
Hatch, William, 131
Havers, Sir Michael, 17
Henlein, Konrad, 58-9
Hewitt, Jack, 100, 103, 124
Hitler, Nazism, 31-3, 49
Hoare, Geoffrey, 122
Hobson, Sir John, 146
Horder, Lord, 31-2
Howard, Brian, 68
Hughes, Richard, 125-7

Inprecorr, 56

Jebb, Sir Gladwyn (later Lord Gladwyn), 90
Jewish Intelligence Services, 53
Jones, R. V., 141

Katz, Otto, 56
Kent, Duke of, 34
Khrushchev, Nikita, 124, 125-6
Klugman, James, 40, 48
Knightley, Philip, 49
Kohlman, Israel, 49
Kohlman, Litzi, *see* Philby, Litzi
Krevitsky, General, 26

Le Carré, John, 21
Leadbitter, Ted, 17, 148
Leitch, David, 49
Lewis, C. Day, 41
Liddell, Guy, 153
'Link', 33
Lipton, Lt-Colonel Marcus, 138, 145-7
Lister, Walter, 133
Llewellyn-Davies, Richard, 69
Lloyd, Selwyn, 60

McAlmon, Robert, 62
Mackenzie, Sir Robert, 89, 90
Maclean, Donald, Sir (father of Donald), 40
Maclean, Donald Duart
　Burgess moved in different circles, 19
　at Cambridge, 33, 35, 39–41
　his communist sympathies, 40–1, 41–2, 52
　his drinking, 63, 74–5, 78, 80–3, 80–7
　his family, childhood, schooling, 40
　his flight with Burgess, 17–18, 20, 94–9, 100–9, 119–27, 129–34, 137–40, 144, 149, 163
　in Foreign Office, 41–2, 50, 76–86 *passim*, 99
　his marriage, *see* Maclean, Melinda
　Moscow life of, 158, 159, 160–1
　not put on trial, 25, 153
　his personality, 44–5, 84
　psychiatric treatment, 83
　his sexual behaviour, 44, 49, 83
　as spy, Russian agent, 26, 27, 77–9, 98–9, 136, 147, 158–9, 165–6
　suspected of spying, 88, 89, 93–5, 97, 167
　'upper-class', 22
　mentioned, 47, 147
Maclean, Donald Fergus (son of Donald Duart), 77, 131
Maclean, Donald Marling (son of Donald Duart), 79
Maclean, Gwendolen, Lady (mother of Donald), 40, 94, 105–6, 121
Maclean, John (grandfather of Donald Duart), 39
Maclean, Melinda (wife of Donald Duart)
　her children, 63, 77, 79, 111
　Donald, meeting and married life, 50, 62–3, 76–7, 79–86
　and flight of Burgess and Maclean, 104–6, 108, 121–3
　joins Donald in Moscow, 113–18, 140
　leaves Donald for Philby, 160
　returns to Donald, 161
Macmillan, Harold, 138–40
Macnamara, Colonel, 53
MacNeice, Louis, 69
McNeil, Hector, 71–2, 75, 76, 95, 156, 159
McNeil, Mrs Hector, 156
Makins, Roger (later Lord Sherfield), 152
Mandrake Club, 74–5
Mann, Dr William, 147
Markov, Georgi, 26
Marlborough College, 22, 34
Marling, Catherine, 62, 111
Marling, Harriet, 62, 80, 81, 111, 112, 117, 118
Marling, Melinda, *see* Maclean, Melinda
'Maurice' (Sir Anthony Blunt, *q.v.*), 18, 147
Maxse, Marjorie, 63–4
May, Alan Nunn, 22–3, 25, 41, 78, 124
Mayall, Lees, 81
Mayor, Theresa, 69
MI5, 27, 28, 32, 60, 67–8, 134, 136, 144, 163
MI6, 28, 69, 87, 88, 140–1, 144, 163–4
Miller, Bernard, 100, 101–2, 103, 104
Miller, John, 131, 132–3
Milmo, Helenus, 137
Molotov, V. M., 126

INDEX

Montagu, Lord, 69
Morrison, Herbert, 28, 79, 96, 102, 139, 158-9
Mosley, Sir Oswald, 33
Mossman, John, 133
Muggeridge, Malcolm, 51
Muir, Robin, 115

Nazism, Hitler, 31-2, 49
Nicolson, Sir Harold, 19, 72, 95
nineteen-thirties, 31-3

Official Secrets Act, 18, 130
Oxford University, communism at, 32, 43

Page, Bruce, 49
Page, Denys, 70
Palmes, Peter, 130
Pembroke College, Cambridge, 46, 52
Petrov, Vladimir, 137
Pfeiffer, Edouard, 56, 57-8
Philby, Aileen (wife of Kim), 69, 87
Philby, Dora (mother of Kim), 37, 50
Philby, Eleanor (wife of Kim), 142, 159-60
Philby (Harold Adrian Russell), Kim
 his birth, parents, childhood, schooling, 36-8
 at Cambridge, 33, 35, 38, 40
 his communist sympathies, 41, 49
 fails to enter Foreign Office, 51
 and flight of Maclean and Burgess, 88, 93, 94-5, 97-9, 100-1, 128, 137-9, 142, 144-6
 his flight to Russia, 141-2
 a journalist, 51, 61, 63, 140
 his marriages, see Philby, Aileen/ Eleanor/Litzi/Nina
 in MI6, 69, 87-8, 89, 140-1, 164
 Moscow life of, 159-61
 not suspected, 167
 not put on trial, 25
 his personality, character, 27-8, 41
 and Section D, 64
 his sexual behaviour, 49
 and SOE, 67, 68-9
 as spy, Russian agent, 26, 28, 41, 49, 51, 61, 87-8, 141-2, 163-5
 suspected, interrogated, 89, 136-7, 140-2
 'upper-class', 22
 in Vienna after leaving Cambridge, 48-9
 mentioned, 19, 29, 47, 166
Philby, Harold St John Bridger (father of Kim), 36-8
Philby, Helena, Patricia and Diana (sisters of Kim), 37
Philby, Litzi (née Kohlman; wife of Kim), 49, 50, 69
Philby, Nina (wife of Kim), 160
Pigou, A. C., 147
Pitt Club, 44
Pontecorvo, Bruno, 78
Price, Christopher, 17
Purdy, Anthony, and Sutherland, Douglas, 18-20, 73, 93, 129, 134, 144, 167
Putlitz, Wolfgang, von, 57, 90

'Q' Section, 29

RAC Club, 94
Reed, John, 70
Rees, Goronwy, 19, 46, 52, 53-4, 55-6, 72-3, 86-7, 103, 156
Reform Club, 74, 94

INDEX

Ribbentrop, Joachim von, 57
Rothschild, Mrs Charles, 53, 57–8
Rothschild, Victor (later Lord Rothschild), 52, 67, 68, 152
Rubinstein, Michael, 17

Saanenmoser, 114
St Ermin's Hotel, 58, 63–4
Section D, 61, 64
Sherfield, Lord, *see* Makins, Roger
Skardon, William, 137, 155
Smith, Det-Supt George Gordon, 130
SOE, 65, 67
Solon, Larry, 120
Special Branch, 29, 30
Spender, Stephen, 100
'Stiles, Roger', 104
Strachey, John, 67–8, 96
Sutherland, Douglas, *see* Purdy and Sutherland

Taylor, A. J. P., 43
Tennant, Hon. David, 75
Territet, 115
Thatcher, Margaret, Blunt named by, 17–18, 147–51
Thomas, Hugh, 67–8
Thompson, 'Tommy', 89–90, 93
Thomson, Admiral, 119–20
Times, The
letter from Lord Horder to, 31–2
letters to, about Melinda Maclean, 123
letter from Mrs Hector McNeil, 156
Tolya, 130, 133
Toynbee, Philip, 43, 81–2
Travellers' Club, 18, 94
Trevelyan, G. M., 46, 54
Trinity College, Cambridge, 34–5, 38, 39, 45
Trinity Hall, Cambridge, 35, 40

Vansittart, Sir Robert (later Lord Vansittart), 57
Vienna, 48–9
Volkov, Konstantin, 70, 164

Warburg Institute, 48, 50
Warner, Sir Fred, 74, 152
Washington
Burgess in, 72, 76, 89–94, 98–9
Maclean in, 77–9, 98–9
Philby, in 88, 89, 164
Watson, Boris, 75
Wedgwood, John, 69
Weidenfeld and Nicolson, 127–8
Westminster School, 22, 37
White, Sir Dick, 137, 40
Wilson, Peter, 153
Windsor, Duke of, 143
Wolfenden, Jeremy, 133

Younger, Kenneth, 95